WEST YORK

RAILWAY STA IONS

Guiseley railway station, which is still in use today.

Pontefract Baghill railway station, taken by John Law *c.* 1981.

WEST YORKSHIRE
RAILWAY STATIONS
From Aberford to Yeadon

PETER TUFFREY

AMBERLEY

Huddersfield railway station from an old print, published by C. H. Johnson, Leeds.

Ilkley railway station staff pose for the camera.

First published 2011

Amberley Publishing
The Hill, Stroud
Gloucestershire, GL5 4EP

www.amberleybooks.com

British Library Cataloguing in Publication Data.
A catalogue record for this book is available from the British Library.

ISBN 978 1 4456 0307 0

Typesetting and Origination by Amberley Publishing.
Printed in Great Britain.

Contents

Acknowledgements

I would like to thank the following people for their help: John Alsop, David Clay, Stephen Gay, John Law, Hugh Parkin, Andrew Stopford, Tristram Tuffrey. Gratitude should also be expressed to Dave at Lost Railways West Yorkshire.

St Dunstan's railway station closed in September 1952.

Introduction

There was a time when research for a railway book could be a massive and tricky undertaking, not disregarding collecting the illustrations. That was no mean task either. Referencing and checking and double checking the facts is absolutely vital because someone will always write to the author or the publisher to dispute a statement.

With the advent of the internet, particularly Amazon and eBay, it is much easier to locate a book or magazine, pay for it online and then have it delivered almost the next day. This, to a certain extent, has done away with ordering a book through a local library, where an anxious wannabe author might be waiting ages for it to arrive only to be told it is for reference use only and cannot be taken away from the library. To augment these internet facilities, Google searches can locate the most esoteric facts and figures about a particular subject, particularly railway stations. Also, *Wikipedia* is run by a marvellous and ever growing group of individuals who post the most remarkable and concise facts on the internet for everyone to use, particularly the 'railway' author.

I first became familiar with West Yorkshire railway stations when I edited and published a smaller work on the subject for Norman Ellis in 1989. Now, in 2011, with the internet facilities at hand, I thought it was time to augment and enlarge this information in a new work on the subject which attempts to include every railway station that has existed in the area.

It was while undertaking a Google search on a particular West Yorkshire railway station that I stumbled upon www.lostrailwayswestyorkshire.co.uk, a most remarkable website. This is run by a man called Dave, along with an army of enthusiasts who have, where possible and whenever allowed, trailed the lost railway routes of West Yorkshire with boundless enthusiasm and documented when these lines were built; where they extended; what they included in terms of track layouts, bridges, signal boxes stations etc.; what has happened to them; and what remains. They have done all this with breathtaking accuracy and presented the facts on a remarkable website. This includes then and now photographs, diagrams and maps. So a hearty slap on the back lads for all your efforts, and for a site that is surely a model for all to follow, particularly when documenting an area's lost railways. I have also used two other sites to gather information: www.railwayramblers.org.uk and www.disused-stations.org.uk, both the result of tireless and inspired efforts of the various members.

For illustrations I have used numerous picture postcards and the archives at the *Yorkshire Post Newspapers*, as well as some noted railway photographers. Among them is Ben Brooksbank, a giant in terms of a railway photographer, who has been active for many years recording the changes to the railway scene, not only in West Yorkshire but throughout the country.

Naturally, the emergence of railway stations in abundance came about with the birth of the railway industry itself, as well as the growth of West Yorkshire as a thriving industrial area. So it was only a natural progression that the communities that grew up alongside it needed transport and stations were quickly provided to facilitate travel.

That being said, railway station architecture never fails to impress or amaze. Many stations date from the early nineteenth century and reflect the grandiose architecture of the time, lending prestige to the city or town as well as to railway operations and operators.

Looking at pictures of stations that have vanished as well as buildings that still exist, the sheer size of them is breathtaking, as is the fine detail they incorporated. Some were almost identical in design. But, while it's hard not to be impressed with the design of old stations, it's equally hard to accept that their statement in architectural terms and the costs of building them were justified. I argue this because some of those in West Yorkshire only existed for a relatively short period. Quite a number were wrongly placed, or were quite a distance from the community they were intending to serve. Many stations were quickly made redundant by the advent of motorbuses and motor vehicles. Some were even built too late to have any use on the railway system they intended to serve.

Another fascinating aspect of railway stations is the sheer numbers of staff they employed. Many staff are seen proudly posing in their uniforms alongside the stationmaster, everyone looking smart and efficient and, probably, equally helpful and amenable. Yet, taking into account the architectural splendour, the volume of staff, and the stations' relatively short lifespan, with some never even seeing a passenger – isn't there an element of the surreal about the entire scene? It would certainly seem that way and maybe that's what Dr Beeching saw in the 1950s and 1960s, providing him with an excuse to wield a large axe and close so many stations.

In gathering together and choosing the pictures for inclusion in this book, I attempted to find a picture of each station mentioned in the A–Z, half knowing at the outset that this would be a futile task as a few stations only lasted a few years. Some even preceded the wide use of cameras and did not even attract an artist's eye to record them. Naturally, some stations were pictured more than others and provide a variety of scenes to be included here.

Instead of merely producing a picture/caption book, I wanted to list every known railway station that existed in West Yorkshire. Because of the enormity of the task and the space available, the information included is kept to a bare minimum. Maybe some more stations will come to light after publication, as new information has a habit of appearing once a book is published. But that it is OK; it can be included when somebody else decides to tackle the subject via some other means besides reference books and the internet.

CHAPTER ONE

Aberford to Burley Park

Addingham railway station facing in the direction of Ilkley.

Aberford railway station

Situated on the Aberford Railway's Garforth–Aberford line (The Aberford Railway or Fly Line), Aberford railway station began passenger services on 3 March 1837. It closed in 1924.

Ackworth railway station

The station was opened by the Swinton and Knottingley Joint Railway on 1 July 1879. Post grouping, the station passed on to the London, Midland & Scottish Railway and London & North Eastern Railway (jointly), then to the Eastern Region of British Railways on nationalisation in 1948. The station was, in effect, closed on 2 July 1951 – but it wasn't official until after 21 July 1959. Although trains pass on the Dearne Valley line, there is no station at Ackworth now. The former goods shed survives and has been converted to a house.

Addingham railway station

Situated on a curve, Addingham railway station was opened by the Midland Railway on 16 May 1888. The main station building was made of stone, and it comprised two platforms. It became part of the London, Midland & Scottish Railway during the Grouping of 1923, passing on to the Eastern Region of British Railways on nationalisation in 1948. The station was closed to passengers by the British Railways Board as part of the Beeching Axe on 22 March 1965 and demolished several years later. The former station site is now a housing estate.

Ackworth railway station.

Altofts railway station; note the timber platforms.

Altofts railway station. (*John Law*)

Altofts railway station

Altofts railway station was opened in 1870 as Altofts and Whitwood by the Midland Railway on its line from Derby to Leeds Wellington Station. The station was built on an embankment using spoil from the cutting south of Normanton; the area was prone to subsidence, resulting in speed restrictions and the need to shore up the platforms. It became part of the London, Midland & Scottish Railway during the Grouping of 1923, later passing on to the Eastern Region of British Railways on nationalisation in 1948. When Sectorisation was introduced in the 1980s, the station was served by Regional Railways under arrangements with the West Yorkshire Passenger Transport Executive. The name 'Whitwood' was dropped in 1970 and the station closed on 14 May 1990; the last day of service was 12 May 1990.

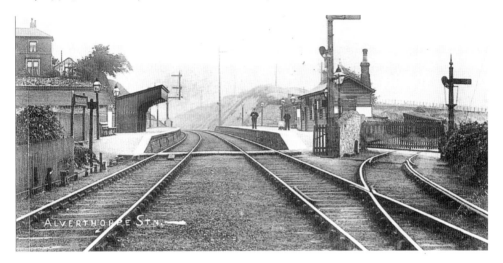

Alverthorpe railway station.

Alverthorpe railway station

Opened by the Great Northern Railway during October 1872, Alverthorpe railway station became part of the London & North Eastern Railway during the Grouping of 1923. The line then passed on to the Eastern Region of British Railways on nationalisation in 1948, and the station closed a mere six years later on 5 April 1954. Nothing now remains on the site.

Appleby Bridge and Rawdon railway station – the platforms.

Apperley Bridge railway station

The Leeds & Bradford, later Midland, line between Leeds and Shipley opened on 30 June 1846 and initially there were no intermediate stations. Thus, temporary ones were quickly provided, including Apperley Bridge, which opened some time during July 1846. A permanent structure followed about a year later. It comprised two platforms, partly covered by an overall roof. The main building ran parallel to the railway on the south side up at road level. About 1900, the station was enlarged to four platforms, with a distinctive wooden building above at road level. The original station building was swept away when a cutting was widened to accommodate the new 'fast lines' on the south side. The station became part of the London, Midland & Scottish Railway during the Grouping of 1923, and then passed to the London Midland Region of British Railways on nationalisation in 1948. It was transferred to the North Eastern Region in 1957 and was finally closed by the British Railways Board on 20 March 1965. The station handled parcels by passenger train right up to the final day.

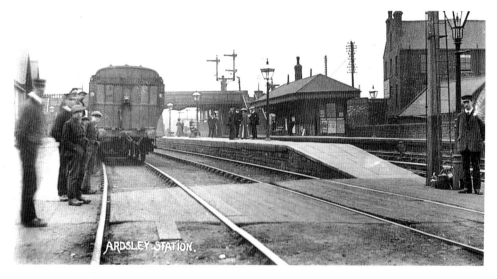

People stand and watch as the photographer takes a panoramic view of Ardsley railway station.

Ardsley railway station

The Bradford, Wakefield & Leeds Railway opened Ardsley railway station on 5 October 1857 as part of their Wakefield–Leeds main line. In time it became part of the Great Northern Railway's rapidly expanding network in the area. By 1866, with the opening of the jointly-owned West Riding & Grimsby Railway from Wakefield to Doncaster, the station was placed on the main line between Leeds and London King's Cross. The station was eventually closed by the British Railways Board on 2 November 1964, with the line to Bradford following suit on 4 July 1966. To the south of the station, east of the main line, was situated the engine shed, which provided the passenger locomotives for the Wakefield services and freight locomotives for the colliery traffic generated in the area. Trains still pass the station site today, though there is little remaining.

Armley Canal Road railway station

Originally named Armley, Armley Canal Road railway station was opened with two platforms by the Leeds & Bradford Railway (subsequently absorbed by the Midland Railway) in 1846. Post-grouping operations were conducted by the London, Midland & Scottish Railway and on 25 September 1950 the station was renamed Armley Canal Road. Closure came on 22 March 1965, though the main station

Right: Arthington railway station with Stationmaster Thomas Imeson on 18 March 1965. (Photograph reproduced by courtesy of *Yorkshire Post* newspapers)

Below: Armley and Wortley railway station, closed in July 1966.

building still survives on Canal Road and is used as commercial premises. Nothing remains of the station at rail level other than the gap between the lines where the island platform formerly stood.

Armley Moor railway station
At first named Armley and Wortley, Armley Moor railway station began services on 1 August 1854 on the former Great Northern Railway between Leeds and Bramley. Post-grouping operations were conducted by the London & North Eastern Railway, the station's name being changed to Armley Moor on 25 September 1950; closure came on 4 July 1966. The station was immortalised in 1964 in the song 'Slow Train' by Flanders and Swann.

Arthington railway station
There have been two stations at Arthington. The original one, sited south of the main road (Arthington Lane), near to the Wharfedale Inn, was opened by the Leeds Northern Railway on 10 April 1849 as 'Pool' and took the 'Arthington' name in February 1852. On 1 February 1865 the station was moved 605 metres south and was built on a triangle with four platforms to serve the Otley branch that opened in 1865. It superseded the first station, which is now a private residence. Post-grouping operations were conducted by the London & North Eastern Railway and closure came during March 1965.

Baildon railway station, looking north.

Baildon railway station
Opened by the Midland Railway on 4 December 1876, Baildon railway station included a single-storey building with two gabled pavilions. It closed on 5 January 1953, but reopened on 28 January 1957. Closing its doors once more on 19 April

1957, it opened once again on 5 January 1973. The station and all trains serving it are operated by Northern Rail.

Bailiff Bridge railway station

Bailiff Bridge railway station, opening on 1 March 1881, was built with two platforms by the Lancashire & Yorkshire Railway and closed on 2 April 1917.

Baildon railway station, 6 January 1973. (Photograph reproduced by courtesy of *Yorkshire Post* newspapers)

Bailiff Bridge railway station with members of the station staff facing the camera.

Bardsey railway station on the North Eastern Railway's Cross Gates–Wetherby branch line.

Bardsey railway station

Bardsey railway station, situated on the North Eastern Railway's 10¼-mile line between Cross Gates (Leeds) and Wetherby, opened on 1 May 1876. Initially a single line, it was doubled in 1902. Bardsey railway station – along with the line – was closed to passengers on 6 January 1964, and goods on 27 April 1964. The station site is now covered with housing.

Batley railway station platform view.

Batley railway station

At one time Batley railway station, 8 miles to the south-west of Leeds, was larger than it is today, being served by the Great Northern Railway branch line from Bradford to Wakefield via Dewsbury Central – it was also the junction for branch lines to Birstall and Tingley. Few traces now remain of these routes. Currently, trains

Batley railway station.

Batley railway station in Great Northern Railway days.

from Batley go towards either Leeds (northbound) or Huddersfield/Hebden Bridge (southbound) on the Huddersfield Line operated by Northern Rail. The station had originally opened in 1848.

Batley Carr railway station
Batley Carr railway station was on the Great Northern Railway Company's line from Ossett (Runtlings Lane Jn) to Batley (Dewsbury Loop), extant between 1874 and 1965; the station opened on 12 April 1880 and closed in 1950. The former site is presently occupied by an auto salvage depot.

Beeston railway station, looking northwards, towards Leeds.

Battyeford railway station

Built by the London & North Western Railway, Battyeford railway station commenced services on 1 October 1900, on the Heaton Lodge–Farnley Junction (Leeds New Line) linking Huddersfield and Leeds via the Spen Valley. The station buildings were of timber construction; the two platforms were brick with stone flags. The station itself was situated at the northern end of Battyeford viaduct, the platforms extending on to the span over the Brighouse–Mirfield road (now the A644). A large goods yard and shed were situated on the Leeds side of the station. Post-grouping operations were conducted by the LMS; the station closed on 3 January 1953 and was subsequently demolished. A substantial remnant of the viaduct remains – apparently it was so well built that the demolition contractors appointed by BR to dismantle the structure gave up.

Beeston railway station

Beeston railway station opened in February 1860 and closed to passengers on 2 March 1953, and to goods on 1 February 1962, though it continued to be used for a time for football specials.

Ben Rhydding railway station

Ben Rhydding railway station was built as part of the Otley & Ilkley Joint Railway, and opened to passenger traffic on 1 July 1866, eleven months after the opening of the railway. In April 1885, the North Eastern Railway Board 'ordered that a small wooden station consisting of booking office, waiting room and retiring room for ladies be provided as a temporary accommodation at Ben Rhydding.' Six years later, in May 1871, the Joint Committee reached an agreement with the proprietor of the Ben Rhydding Hydro that a more permanent station structure should be built at the expense of the Hydro. The Hydro's arrangements with the company lasted until 1885, when the structures – a stone-built station house on the south (down) platform and a wooden structure on the north (up) platform – were sold to the railway company for £240. Station staff were withdrawn on 7 October 1968, when 'pay-trains' were introduced. The stone station building has subsequently been demolished, and shelter on both platforms is restricted to simple bus-stop type covered areas. Ben Rhydding is currently served by Class 333 electric trains run by Northern Rail, who also manage the station.

Ben Rhydding railway station photographed on 19 October 1955, after winning British Railways' Best Kept Station competition. From left to right: Station Porter, F. Lupton; Stationmaster N. Darby; and Porter/Signalman E. Thackray. (Photograph reproduced courtesy of *Yorkshire Post* newspapers)

Berry Brow railway station

The original Berry Brow station was 300 metres from the present location, in the direction of Huddersfield, opening on 1 July 1850 and closing 2 July 1966. The present single-platform station was opened 9 October 1989 and lies some 2¼ miles south of Huddersfield railway station on the Penistone Line between Huddersfield and Sheffield – it is managed by Northern Rail.

Berry Brow railway station, looking north-west towards Huddersfield, on 22 April 1961. (*Ben Brooksbank*)

Bingley railway station

Bingley railway station was opened by the Leeds & Bradford Railway, on their Leeds & Bradford Extension Railway line from Shipley to Keighley, on 16 March 1847. Initially the station was built of wood, but the Midland Railway (who had absorbed the L&BR in 1851) opened the present station on 24 July 1892. It is about 400 yards south of the original station. Currently the station is managed by Northern Rail and there are two platforms in use.

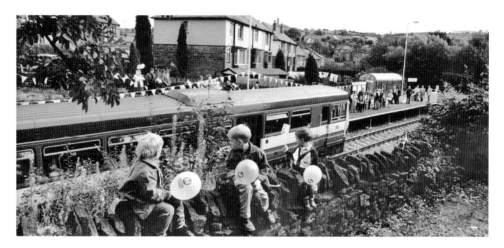

The new railway station at Berry Brow on the first day of opening, 9 October 1989. (Photograph reproduced courtesy of *Yorkshire Post* newspapers)

Birkenshaw & Tong railway station

Birkenshaw & Tong railway station was on the Great Northern Railway's Ardsley–Laisterdyke (Bradford) line; a stretch of 10¼ miles. The station opened on 20 August 1856 and closed 3 October, 1953.

The old Bingley railway station on the final day of services, July 1892.

The new Bingley railway station that opened on 24 July 1892.

Birstall Lower railway station
Birstall Lower railway station was on the London & North Western Railway's Batley–Birstall single-track branch line, stretching two miles, and opened on 30 September 1852. The station closed 1 January 1917, partially due to competition from trams – the site was eventually cleared.

Birstall Upper railway station (later Birstall Town)
The buildings and platforms were of timber construction, with a subway at Birstall Upper railway station that opened on 1 October 1900. The station was renamed Birstall Town in 1935 and closed on 1 August 1951.

Bower's Halt railway station
Bower's Halt railway station was on the North Eastern Railway's Castleford East Jn–Garforth line and opened on 12 August 1878. It closed on 22 January 1951 and no trace remains.

Bowling railway station
Bowling railway station opened on 1 August 1854 and closed on 1 February 1895.

Bowling Junction railway station
Bowling Junction railway station opened on 1 February 1902 and pre-grouping operations were conducted by the L&Y Railway. The station closed on 3 December 1951.

It was situated on the Caldervale line to the south of Bradford Exchange.

The remains of Bowling Junction railway station, looking southwards towards Low Moor on 22 April 1961. (*Ben Brooksbank*)

Bradford Adolphus Street

The Leeds, Bradford & Halifax Junction Railway initially built a station at Adolphus Street, Bradford, which opened on 1 August 1854. But being poorly situated, a link line was constructed from east of the terminus, looping south and joining the existing Lancashire & Yorkshire line at Mill Lane Junction, allowing LB&HJ services to enter Bradford Exchange station. As a result, Adolphus Street station was closed to passengers in 1867, closing completely in the 1960s and was later demolished.

Birkenshaw and Tong railway station, closed in 1953.

Bradford Exchange railway station. (Photograph reproduced courtesy of *Yorkshire Post* newspapers)

Bradford Exchange railway station, 29 July 1973. (Photograph reproduced courtesy of *Yorkshire Post* newspapers)

Bradford Exchange and Bradford Interchange

The original Bradford Exchange railway station was opened by the joint efforts of the Lancashire & Yorkshire Railway and the Great Northern Railway on 9 May 1850. The station was completely rebuilt on the same site in 1880 with ten platforms, in a similar style to London King's Cross with two arched roofs. Around 1973, the station was rebuilt once more, but on a different site slightly further south. The old Exchange station was demolished soon afterwards; the site now houses Bradford Crown Court.

In 1977 a bus station was built alongside, and in 1983 the new station was re-named Bradford Interchange to link buses and trains in a covered environment.

Bradford Interchange railway station, July 1981. (Photograph reproduced courtesy of *Yorkshire Post* newspapers)

Bradford Market Street railway station's arcaded façade.

Bradford Forster Square railway station

For this station's early history, please see Bradford Market Street.

Wikipedia states that by 1906, Forster Square had been built just south-east of the station, but the name Forster Square Station was not used until 1924. The current Forster Square Station, a modern three-platform station, was built in 1990, slightly to the north of the former station; the latter was demolished, but part of the screen arcade that fronted the 1890 station remains, as does the Midland Hotel.

Bradford Forster Square railway station, 19 October 1962. (Photograph reproduced courtesy of *Yorkshire Post* newspapers)

Entrance to Bradford Forster Square railway station, 19 October 1962. (Photograph reproduced courtesy of *Yorkshire Post* newspapers)

Bradford Forster Square railway station in the spring of 1999. (*John Law*)

The original Bradford Market Street railway station.

Bradford Market Street

The Bradford railway station that was at one time called Market Street can trace its history back to the 1840s and to a building on Kirkgate, opposite the end of Market Street. It is claimed this building was an imposing neo-classical structure designed by William Andrews.

Interior view of Bradford Market Street railway station looking north.

By 1853, the Midland Railway had rebuilt the station; the new building was larger, but apparently less interesting architecturally. In 1890 the station was again replaced. The Midland Railway's architect, Charles Trubshaw, designed a large complex containing the passenger station, goods station and the Midland Hotel. The station had six platforms and an overall glazed roof of the ridge and furrow pattern. *Wikipedia* states there is some disagreement about what names – Market

Street or Forster Square – were used for the stations and when: 'Most of the modern references state that one or more of them were called "Market Street", though there is disagreement as to exactly when this name was in use: Sheeran, George (1994) *Railway Buildings of West Yorkshire, 1812–1920* says it was "Market Street" from the rebuilding in 1890 until 1924. Tony Dewick's *Complete Atlas of Railway Station Names* (2002) p. 42 shows one of the three stations as "Market Street" in red, which in that book indicates that the station and the name passed out of use before 1901.'

Wikipedia also points out that contemporary sources do not seem to use a name for the station. 'The Bradford Post Office Directory says that the Midland terminal is at "Station, bottom of Kirkgate" (1856, 1863, 1898) or "Station, Forster Square" (1916, 1927); only in 1928 did a directory use the name "Forster Square Station". In contrast, from 1879/80 onward the directories show the other terminal as "Exchange Station, Drake St". It seems likely that the original station was called simply 'Bradford', at least until the Lancashire & Yorkshire station opened at Drake Street in 1850. After that time it would have been the Midland Station. At some time it apparently came to be called "Bradford Market Street", but this does not appear to have been official.'

Bradley railway station
Bradley railway station opened in 1847, along the first section of the new Huddersfield & Manchester Railway, but was resited two years later. The station closed in 1952.

Bramley railway station, facing eastwards.

Bramley railway station
Bramley railway station, with platforms opposite each other and connected by a footbridge, opened on 1 August 1854. The station closed on 2 July 1966. The present station off Stanningley Road was opened on 12 September 1983 by Metro (West Yorkshire Passenger Transport Executive).

Bramley railway station entrance, with the goods yard to the right.

Scene at the official reopening of Bramley railway station on 12 September 1983. (Photograph reproduced by courtesy of *Yorkshire Post* newspapers)

Brighouse railway station

Brighouse railway station was first opened in October 1840, as a main line station operated by the Manchester & Leeds Railway. The station was initially known as Brighouse for Bradford, as no stations had been built at that period in Bradford itself. Pre-grouping operations were conducted by the Lancashire & Yorkshire Railway, post-grouping by the London, Midland & Scottish Railway. The station was eventually closed by British Rail in January 1970, but reopened on Sunday 28 May 2000.

Brighouse railway station looking westwards, towards Halifax and Manchester, on 22 April 1961. (*Ben Brooksbank*)

Brighouse Clifton Road railway station

Brighouse Clifton Road railway station was built with two platforms by the Lancashire & Yorkshire Railway on their Pickle Bridge line from Anchor Pit Junction east of Brighouse (on the Manchester & Leeds Calder Valley main line) via Clifton Road and Bailiff Bridge to Pickle Bridge Junction near Wyke (on the Halifax–Bradford line) on 1 March 1881. Post grouping operations were conducted by the Midland Railway and the station closed on 14 September 1931. It was demolished three years later.

Brockholes railway station, facing north-westwards towards Huddersfield, on 22 April 1961. (*Ben Brooksbank*)

Brockholes railway station

Brockholes railway station near Huddersfield was formerly the junction for the Holmfirth Branch Line, which was closed to passenger trains on 2 November 1959, and to goods trains in 1965. Dating back to 1 July 1850, the station is currently on the Penistone line operated by Northern Rail.

Brockholes railway station.

Burley-in-Wharfedale railway station, facing in the direction of Ilkley.

Burley-in-Wharfedale railway station

Burley-in-Wharfedale railway station, in the City of Bradford Metropolitan District, opened in 1865 on the North Eastern Railway/Midland Railway Joint Otley–Burley-in-Wharfedale line. The station's name was changed from Burley to Burley-in-Wharfdale in 1922 and it has been unstaffed since October 1968. Demolition work occurred there in 1973, and it is now managed by Northern Rail.

Burley Park railway station

Burley Park railway station is the first stop on the Harrogate Line, 2¼ miles north-west of Leeds railway station towards Harrogate and York – it was opened on 28 November 1988. The station occasionally plays the role of 'Hotten railway station' in the TV series *Emmerdale*.

CHAPTER TWO

Calverley to Frizinghall

Calverley and Rodley railway station, facing eastwards.

Calverley and Rodley railway station

Calverley and Rodley railway station, built by the Leeds & Bradford Railway on their Leeds–Bradford line, opened in July 1846 and closed to passengers in 1965 and goods in 1968.

Carlinghow railway station

Carlinghow railway station was on the London & North Western Railway's Batley–Birstall Lower (goods) line and opened on 1 April 1872. The *Lost Railways of West Yorkshire* website states the following details about the station:

> The location of Carlinghow station is approximately 10 to 50 yards from the bridge support on Carlinghow Hill (Birstall side of the bridge) and I recall seeing it many times as I went to Batley General Hospital which is now a Nursing Home. It was accessible by the drive up to the Hospital. It was stone built and was probably on the left hand side of the track as you would walk to Birstall. Its length was not long at best 100 feet complete with two ramps, very much a halt type station.

The station closed on 1 January 1917.

Castleford railway station, which replaced an earlier station.

Castleford railway station

The original Castleford railway station was built by the York & North Midland Railway on their line from York to Normanton and opened on 1 July 1840. The current Castleford railway station was built by the North Eastern Railway in 1871 to replace the earlier one that had been 400 metres to the east of the new location. By the end of the nineteenth century, the new station (by now known as Castleford Central) had an impressive range of services to choose from, with regular links to Leeds, Wakefield and on towards Manchester Victoria through the Calder Valley, as well as to York. Longer distance destinations (including Sheffield, Derby, Birmingham and London) were also available by means of a change at Normanton. By the early 1950s, however, the local network began to decline and although originally built as a through station, regular passenger services beyond Castleford towards York were discontinued in January 1970. Today, Castleford is currently an unstaffed station and all services reverse there, arriving and departing from a single platform. Freight traffic runs through the station.

Castleford Cutsyke railway station

Castleford Cutsyke (renamed Castleford Cutsyke in 1952) railway station was opened by the Lancashire & Yorkshire Railway on their line from Castleford Cutsyke Junction to Methley Junction in 1860 and closed on 7 October 1968. Currently, only one concrete platform remains of the station.

Chickenley Heath railway station

The Great Northern Railway opened Chickenley Heath railway station on their line from Wrenthorpe South Junction to Adwalton Junction in 1877. The station closed on 1 July 1909.

Churwell railway station

Churwell railway station opened on 10 September 1848 and closed on 2 December 1940.

A rare shot of Chickenley Heath railway station on the Great Northern Railway's Ossett–Batley branch line.

Churwell railway station about 1930, with Snittles' Farm in the background.

Clayton railway station

Clayton railway station was on the Great Northern Railway lines to Bradford, Keighley and Halifax via Queensbury, collectively known as the Queensbury Lines, and opened on 14 October 1878. The station had an island platform and a reasonable goods yard, but closed in 1955 and houses have since been erected on the site.

Clayton West railway station

Clayton West railway station was opened on 1 September 1879 by the Lancashire & Yorkshire railway. It was closed on 24 January 1983 and now forms the eastern terminus of the Kirklees Light Railway.

Cleckheaton Central railway station

Cleckheaton Central railway was originally constructed with two platforms by the Lancashire & Yorkshire Railway, on their Mirfield to Low Moor (Cleckheaton Branch) line in 1847. The last passenger train working was the service from Bradford on 12 June 1965, arriving at Cleckheaton at 11.21 p.m.; the station closed to freight traffic some four years later. Cleckheaton Central railway station has the distinction of being the

Clayton West railway station, spring 1989. (*John Law*)

Cleckheaton Central railway station, looking towards Heckmondwike. (*Bernard Coomber*)

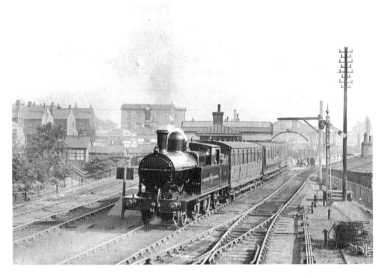

An L&Y 2-4-2T at Cleckheaton railway station, which closed in 1965.

only British railway station to have been 'stolen'. In 1972, a Dewsbury man appeared at Wakefield Crown Court; in the words of the prosecution counsel, 'What the case really comes to is that this man last August in effect stole Cleckheaton station.' British Rail had contracted him for the clearing of the site in August 1971, part of the deal being that the contractors would sell, and retain the proceeds from disposal of, the materials and scrap. On arrival, they discovered that the station and most of the material were already gone. It transpired that the man had been contracted by another firm to clear the site, had been advanced a sum for hire of plant, and had spent three weeks clearing the site. Subsequent efforts to trace the second firm failed, and the court found the man not guilty, deciding that he had been duped and left significantly out of pocket.

Cleckheaton Spen railway station
Cleckheaton Spen railway station was on the London & North Western Railway's Spen Valley Jn–Leeds (Farnley Branch Jn) line and opened on 1 October 1900. Sir Winston Churchill, then Prime Minister, slept at Cleckheaton Spen sidings overnight in a special train with a heavy security cordon during election campaigning in 1952. Cleckheaton Spen railway station closed on 5 January 1953 and was later demolished.

Clifton Road railway station
Clifton Road railway station, situated on the Lancashire & Yorkshire Railway's Brighouse (Anchor Pit Jn)–Wike Jn (Pickle Bridge Branch) line, opened on 1 March 1881. It closed in 1931 and no trace remains.

Cockden railway station
Cockden railway station is mentioned on Malcolm Bulls's Calderdale Companion website as serving the mills between Callis and Woodhouse. No opening or closure dates are mentioned.

Collingham Bridge railway station, closed 1964.

Collingham Bridge railway station

Collingham Bridge railway station comprised two platforms and was opened on the North Eastern Railway's Cross Gates–Wetherby East Jn line on 1 May 1876. The station was closed on 6 January 1964 and the site redeveloped for housing.

Cooper Bridge railway station

Huddersfield's Cooper Bridge railway station, which included an island platform, was built by the Lancashire & Yorkshire Railway on their Calder Valley main line (Manchester–Normanton), opening in 1840. It was Huddersfield's first railway station and post-grouping operations were conducted by the London, Midland & Scottish Railway; the station closed on 20 February 1950.

Copley railway station, facing west.

Copley railway station building and platform.

Copley railway station

Copley railway station was opened in November 1855 by the Lancashire & Yorkshire Railway. The station buildings were largely constructed of wood and it had two platforms. Post-grouping operations were conducted by the London, Midland & Scottish Railway; the station closed on 20 July 1931.

Cornholme railway station, facing in a westerly direction.

Cornholme railway station

Opened on the Copy Pit line by the Lancashire & Yorkshire Railway in July 1878, Cornholme railway station had two platforms and was closed by the LMS on 26 September 1938. The line remains in use for passenger trains between York/Leeds and Blackpool, which run non-stop between Hebden Bridge and Burnley.

Cottingley railway station

With financial assistance from West Yorkshire Passenger Transport Executive, Cottingley railway station was opened in May 1988. It is currently managed by Northern Rail, providing all passenger services.

Crigglestone East railway station

Crigglestone East railway station on the Midland Railway's Royston Jn–Thornhill Midland Jn (Middlestown Branch) line opened on 10 November 1905 for goods. The station was originally planned as a passenger station and closed in 1964. The former site of the station is now occupied by a golf club.

Crigglestone West railway station

Crigglestone West railway station opened on 1 January 1850 on the Wakefield–Barnsley line and closed on 13 September 1965.

Crigglestone railway station, the sign board clearly visible on the left.

Crofton railway station, situated between Wakefield and Pontefract.

Crofton railway station

Crofton railway station opened on 1 November 1853 and closed on 30 November 1931. *Wikipedia* states:

> A smaller station at Crofton was located next to Doncaster road, on the current Pontefract Line, behind the Crofton Arms public house. The station was demolished in the 1960s, yet the remains of the old station house in its current derelict form can be seen from the A638, or on passing trains from Wakefield Kirkgate railway station towards Pontefract.

Crossflatts railway station

Crossflatts railway station, Bingley, was opened on 17 May 1982. It was the first of the eighties-era stations on the Airedale line to be opened, and is the only one to be built on an entirely new site (the others – such as Saltaire & Frizinghall – had all previously been closed in 1965 as part of the Beeching cuts). Two platforms are in use and the station is managed by Northern Rail.

A busy scene on the platform at Cross Gates railway station.

Cross Gates railway station staff.

Cross Gates railway station

Cross Gates railway station, on the Leeds–Selby line, opened in 1834 and is currently operated by Northern Rail. In the past signwriters have been unsure as to the correct spelling of Cross Gates, The have put 'Cross Gates' on the westbound platform and 'Crossgates' on the eastbound platform. The correct spelling remains open, but as of 2010, only the 'Cross Gates' spelling is shown. Until 1963, passenger services existed between Cross Gates and Wetherby railway station. The Cross Gates–Wetherby line was closed under the Beeching Axe. Alternative routes to Scarborough existed along this line, as well as raceday specials to Wetherby racecourse.

Cullingworth railway station, looking south.

Cullingworth railway station

Cullingworth railway station on the Great Northern Railway's Queensbury–Keighley line was opened on 7 April 1884. The station closed on 23 May 1955, though freight facilities were provided until 1963. The site was subsequently cleared and is presently occupied by an industrial unit.

Cullingworth railway station, facing north.

Damems railway station

The Midland Railway originally opened Damems railway station on 1 September 1867, and it had the distinction of being a station rather than a halt. This is because in its original form it included a stationmaster's house and a siding to serve the mill in the village. Largely constructed of wood, the structure depicted was eventually bought by a farmer for use as a hen hut! Damems closed on 23 May 1949 – some years before the line itself closed – but reopened with the line on 29 June 1968. It claims to be Britain's smallest railway station, although it is not part of the main British rail network anymore, being managed by the Keighley & Worth Valley Railway.

The small buildings at Damems railway station that later became a hen house.

Scene at the opening of Deighton railway station on 26 April 1982.

Deighton railway station

Deighton railway station, near Huddersfield, opened on 30 August 1871 and closed on 28 July 1930. A new Deighton railway station was opened with two platforms on 26 April 1982 by Metro (the West Yorkshire Passenger Transport Executive) close to the earlier station.

Denby Dale and Cumberworth railway station, facing north.

Denby Dale and Cumberworth railway station

Denby Dale and Cumberworth railway station opened on the Huddersfield & Sheffield Junction Railway between Huddersfield and Penistone on 1 July 1850. The structure was mainly of wood, though now it only has one platform with a solitary shelter and is managed by Northern Rail.

Denholme railway station was at one time the 'highest' on the GNR network.

Denholme railway station

Denholme railway station on the Great Northern Railway's Keighley–Queensbury section of the Queensbury Lines was opened on 1 January 1884. It was situated 850 feet above sea level and had an island platform that was accessed by a long iron footbridge spanning the goods yard. The station closed on 23 May 1955 and is currently the site of a timber yard.

Denholme railway station, which had an island platform accessed by a long iron footbridge spanning the goods yard.

Dewsbury Central railway station

Dewsbury Central railway station was on the Great Northern Railway's Ossett (Runtlings Lane Jn)–Batley (Dewsbury Loop) line and opened on 9 September 1874. The station was renamed Central in 1951 and closed in 1964. The station façade can still be seen, as it was incorporated into a bridge supporting the Dewsbury Ring Road in 1985.

Dewsbury Market Place railway station

Dewsbury Market Place railway station, formerly operated by the Lancashire & Yorkshire Railway, began passenger services on 1 April 1867. It closed on 1 December 1930.

Dewsbury Thornhill railway station

Dewswbury Thornhill railway station was the first passenger station to arrive in Dewsbury, being built by the Manchester & Leeds Railway and opened as Dewsbury on 5 October 1840. The name was changed to Thornhill in January 1851 and the station closed on 1 January 1962.

Dewsbury Central railway station was situated above street level and closed in 1964.

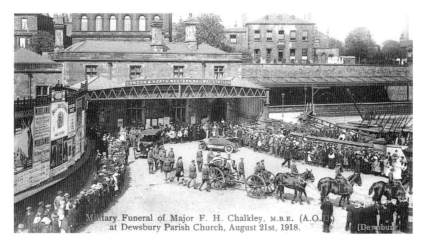

Exterior view of Dewsbury Wellington Road railway station on 21 August 1918, at the time of the funeral of Major F. H. Chalkley.

Dewsbury Wellington Road railway station, the town's only surviving station, 3 February 1993. (Photograph reproduced courtesy of *Yorkshire Post* newspapers)

Dewsbury Market Place railway station, which existed between 1867 and 1930.

Dewsbury (Wellington Road) railway station

Originally known as Dewsbury Wellington Road, Dewsbury railway station was opened in 1848 by the London & North Western Railway. Presently managed by TransPennine Express trains, the station provides a stop between Leeds and Huddersfield. The station is on the Huddersfield Line operated by Northern Rail.

Drighlington and Adwalton railway station

Drighlington and Adwalton railway station was on the Leeds, Bradford & Halifax Junction Railway's Ardsley–Laisterdyke line and opened on 20 August 1856. It closed on 30 December 1961.

Dudley Hill railway station

Dudley Hill railway station was on the Leeds, Bradford & Halifax Junction Railway's Ardsley–Laisterdyke line and opened on 20 August 1856, closing on 1 October 1875. A resited station at Dudley was opened on 1 October 1875 and closed to passengers on 7 April 1952.

Earlsheaton railway station

The Great Northern Railway opened Earlsheaton railway station on the Ossett (Runtlings Lane Jn)–Batley (Dewsbury Loop) line in January 1875. The station was at a lower level than the village, so when leaving the station passengers had to make a steep climb before continuing forwards. The last train called at the station on 6 June 1953 and it was subsequently demolished, though the site is unused today.

East Garforth railway station

Metro (West Yorkshire Passenger Transport Executive) opened East Garforth railway station on 1 May 1987 to serve the new housing developments in the area. The station is an unstaffed halt, has wooden platforms, lies on the York and Selby lines and is operated by Northern Rail, and the westbound platform buildings house the West Riding Licensed Refreshment Rooms.

East Garforth railway station, 22 April 1991.

Earlsheaton railway station, which closed to passengers in 1953.

Eastwood railway station

Eastwood railway station was opened by the Manchester & Leeds Railway on 1 January 1841. Pre-grouping operations were conducted by the Lancashire & Yorkshire Railway, post-grouping by the London, Midland & Scottish Railway, the station closing on 3 December 1951.

Eccleshill railway station

Eccleshill railway station, with two platforms, was opened by the Great Northern Railway on their Bradford (Laisterdyke East Jn)–Shipley line on 15 April 1875. The station closed on 2 February 1931 and there is no trace left.

Eccleshill railway station, facing south.

Elland railway station

The Manchester & Leeds railway opened Elland railway station on their Calder Valley main line (Manchester–Normanton) on 5 October 1840. The station was resited on 1 August 1865 and closed on 10 September 1962.

Esholt railway station with train approaching.

Esholt railway station

Esholt railway station, with two platforms, began passenger services on 4 December 1876 on the Shipley–Guiseley line of the Midland Railway, and closed on 28 October 1940.

Farnley and Wortley railway station
Farnley and Wortley railway station opened on 8 October 1848 and closed on 3 November 1952.

Featherstone railway station
Featherstone railway station began passenger services on 1 April 1848 and closed on 2 February 1967. The present station was opened by Metro (West Yorkshire Passenger Transport Executive) on 12 May 1992, when the line between Wakefield and Pontefract was re-opened. It lies on the Pontefract Line, operated by Northern Rail, 6 miles east of Wakefield Kirkgate railway station.

Featherstone railway station closed in 1967.

The new Featherstone railway station, 29 December 1997. (Photograph reproduced by courtesy of *Yorkshire Post* newspapers)

Fenay Bridge & Lepton railway station
Fenay Bridge railway station was located on the London & North Western Railway's Kirkburton branch line and opened on 7 October 1867. The station was renamed Fenay Bridge & Lepton in 1897; closure came on 28 July 1930, and now no trace remains.

Ferrybridge railway station, facing north.

Ferrybridge railway station

Ferrybridge railway station was opened with two platforms on 1 May 1882 by the North Eastern Railway. From Ferrybridge, stations such as Pontefract Baghill and Ackworth could be reached, as well as other stations to Sheffield. Heading north, stations such as Milford Junction, Monk Fryston and Burton Salmon could be reached, as well as other stations to York. Ferrybridge railway station closed on 13 September 1965.

Fitzwilliam railway station

The original Fitzwilliam railway station was situated a short distance further north from the present station, which opened on 1 March 1982. The new station is on the Wakefield line operated by Northern Rail. Trains ran from Fitzwilliam to Leeds via Wakefield Westgate, Doncaster and Sheffield. The old station was opened by the London & North Eastern Railway on 1 June 1937 and closed on 6 November 1967.

Fitzwilliam railway station, photographed late 1983. (*John Law*)

Flushdyke railway station existed 1862–1941.

Flushdyke railway station

After being opened on 7 April 1862 by the Bradford, Wakefield & Leeds Railway on the Adwalton Junction to Wakefield line, Flushdyke railway station survived until 5 May 1941.

The original Frizinghall railway station.

Frizinghall railway station

Frizinghall railway station was opened with two platforms opposite each other on the north side of Frizinghall Road by the Midland Railway on 1 February 1875. It remained in operation until it was closed on 20 March 1965, a casualty of the Beeching Axe. However, the line on which it stood remained open, and on 7 September 1987 the West Yorkshire Passenger Transport Executive reopened the station. The current station has two platforms, but they're separated: the northbound platform is approximately where it was before, and the southbound is to the south of Frizinghall Road. Bradford Grammar School was relocated to Frizinghall in the late 1940s. From then until closure, and again after reopening, pupils have constituted one of the main sources of traffic at the station. Indeed, it was an English teacher at Bradford Grammar School, Dr Robin Sisson, who actively fought for Frizinghall station to reopen.

CHAPTER THREE

Garforth to Ingrow

Garforth railway station on the Leeds–Selby line.

Garforth railway station
Garforth railway station near Leeds was opened by the Leeds and Selby Railway in 1834. Presently there are two platforms in use and Northern Rail operates services to Leeds, with most services going beyond towards Bradford Interchange, as well as services to York and Selby to the east. First TransPennine Express trains also stop at Garforth hourly towards Leeds, Huddersfield and Manchester Airport (Liverpool Lime Street on Sundays) westbound and York and Middlesbrough (Scarborough on Sundays) eastbound.

Garforth, East railway station (see East Garforth)

Gildersome East railway station
The London & North Western Railway opened Gildersome East railway station (also known as Gildersome St Bernard's) on their Heaton Lodge–Farnley Junction (Leeds New line) on 1 October 1900. The station survived until 11 July 1921 and no trace remains.

Gildersome West railway station
Gildersome West railway station was opened on the Leeds, Bradford & Halifax Junction Railway's Ardsley–Laisterdyke line on 20 August 1856. Closure came on 13 June 1955 for passengers and 13 March 1968 for freight.

Gildersome railway station, looking west.

Glasshoughton railway station

Glasshoughton railway station lies on the Pontefract line operated by Northern Rail. The station is a new one on the network and was opened by Metro (West Yorkshire Passenger Transport Executive) on 21 February 2005.

Gomersall railway station

Gomersall railway station was on the London & North Western Railway's Heaton Lodge–Farnley Junction (Leeds New Line) and opened on 1 October 1900. The station was situated next to the eastern entrance to Gomersall tunnel and the platforms and buildings were of timber construction. Closure came on 5 October 1953 and nothing of the station remains.

Golcar railway station

Golcar railway station, located between the existing Huddersfield and Slaithwaite stations, was opened with four platforms by the London & North Western Railway on 1 August 1849. Along with several other stations on this stretch of line, it was closed to passengers in 1968.

Great Horton railway station

Great Horton railway station, on the Queensbury–Bradford section of the Queensbury Lines, was opened by the Great Northern Railway on 14 October 1878. The station

Gomersall railway station, facing east.

Great Horton railway station, situated on the east side of Beckside Road.

closed on 23 May 1955 to passengers, but remained open to goods with a full staff for several years before it was closed and the tracks ripped up. The station has since been demolished, and a bathroom factory and industrial park now stands on the site.

Greetland & North Dean railway station

Greetland & North Dean railway station was originally opened with two platforms by the Manchester & Leeds Railway as North Dean in July 1844. The station name was subsequently changed to North Dean and Greetland, and then to Greetland in 1897. Situated near the junction of the main Calder Valley line and the steeply-graded branch towards Halifax, it also served as the junction station for the Stainland branch from its opening in 1875 until 1929. Greetland & North Dean was closed to passenger traffic on 10 September 1962 and demolished several years later.

Greetland and North Dean railway station existed between 1844 and 1962.

Guiseley railway station on the Wharfedale line.

Guiseley railway station

Guiseley railway station began services on 1 August 1865 and currently has two platforms in use. It is on the Wharfedale line between Ilkley and Leeds/Bradford Forster Square and served mostly by Class 333 electric trains run by Northern Rail, which also manages the station. Facilities were redeveloped in 2002 to give a new waiting room on platform 2 (for trains to Leeds and Bradford) and a waiting room and ticket office on platform 1 (for trains to Ilkley).

Haigh railway station

Haigh railway station opened on 1 January 1850 and closed on 13 September 1965.

Halifax railway station

Halifax railway station, opened on 7 August 1850, lies on the Caldervale line and is 17 miles west from Leeds. Halifax station is an example of a single island platform acting

Haigh railway station.

Approach to Halifax railway station.

Halifax railway station, built by the L&Y in conjunction with the GNR.

as two platforms. Platform 2 heads eastbound, towards Bradford while platform 1 heads westbound towards Brighouse, Huddersfield, Sowerby Bridge and Manchester Victoria.

Halifax North Bridge railway station
Located on the Halifax & Ovenden Junction Railway (Holmfield to Halifax), Halifax North Bridge railway station was opened with two platforms on 25 March 1880. Pre-grouping operations were conducted by the Lancashire & Yorkshire Railway and Great Northern Railway, post-grouping by the London, Midland & Scottish Railway and the London & North Eastern Railway. It closed to passengers on 23 May 1955 and has since been demolished, with a leisure centre built on the site.

Halifax St Paul's railway station
The short-lived Halifax High Level Railway (Holmfield to St Pauls) was built jointly by the Great Northern and Lancashire & Yorkshire Railway to serve the west side of

Halifax North Bridge railway station closed in 1955.

Halifax. Halifax St Paul's railway station opened on the line on 5 September 1890. The branch and its two stations closed to passengers on 1 January 1917 as a wartime economy measure. After 1917, it was a freight only line, which finally closed in June 1960, when Holmfield station closed.

Halifax Shaw Syke railway station
Halifax Shaw Dyke railway station opened on 1 July 1844 and closed on 7 August 1850.

Hare Park & Crofton railway station
Hare Park & Crofton railway station, sometimes just known as Crofton, was on the West Riding & Grimsby Railway, and began passenger services in November 1885. It was closed on 31 March 1952.

Hare Park and Crofton railway station.

Haworth Station railway station

Haworth railway station was opened in 1867, along with the rest of the Keighley & Worth Valley Railway, and closed in 1962. It re-opened with the preservation of the line in 1968, and now serves as the headquarters of the Keighley & Worth Valley Railway.

Haworth railway station.

Headingley railway station

Headingley railway station, which has also been known as Headingley and Kirkstall railway station, opened in 1849. Currently, the station has two platforms and is managed by Northern Rail.

Headingley railway station, 4 May 1994. (Photograph courtesy of *Yorkshire Post* newspapers)

Healey House railway station

Healey House railway station, on the Lancashire & Yorkshire Railway's Meltham branch line, opened on 5 July 1869 and closed on 23 May 1949. No trace of the station remains.

Healey House railway station.

Heaton Lodge railway station

Heaton Lodge railway station, situated on the London & North Western Railway's Spen Valley Jn–Leeds (Farnley Branch Jn) line, opened to passengers on 1 October 1900. It closed in 1964 and was demolished.

Hebden Bridge railway station

Hebden Bridge railway station was opened in 1840 by the Manchester & Leeds Railway as a terminus station. The opening of the Summit Tunnel in 1841 saw trains continue through to Todmorden, and onwards to Littleborough. Trains began operating to Halifax and Bradford in 1854. Hebden Bridge's current buildings date from 1893, construction having started in 1891. In 1997 the station was renovated, and signage in the original Lancashire & Yorkshire Railway style was erected. The station has two platforms in use and is managed by Northern Rail.

Hebden Bridge railway station, photographed in the late 1980s. (*John Law*)

Heckmondwike Central railway station

Heckmondwike Central railway station was situated on the Lancashire & Yorkshire Railway's Mirfield–Low Moor (Cleckheaton Branch) line and opened 18 July 1848.

It was rebuilt in 1889 and renamed Heckmondwike Central from 1924–61. Closure to passengers came on 14 June 1965, and to freight in May 1969. The Spen Valley Greenway now runs through the site.

Heckmondwike Central railway station.

Heckmondwike Spen railway station

Heckmondwike Spen railway station was opened on the London & North Western Railway's Heaton Lodge–Farnley Junction (Leeds New Line) on 1 October 1900. It was re-named Heckmondwike Spen in 1924 and closed to passengers on 5 October 1953, and completely on 24 August 1964. After the Leeds New Line closed as a through route, British Rail built a connection from the former L&Y line at Heckmondwike to allow trains to get to the Charrington Hargreaves oil terminal which had been built on the site of Liversedge Spen goods depot. These trains ceased in the late 1980s. The station buildings have been demolished, and houses now occupy the site.

Hemsworth railway station.

Hemsworth railway station

Hemsworth railway station, built of brick, was opened by the West Riding & Grimsby Railway on 1 February 1866 and closed on 6 November 1967. The main station building had a hipped roof and turret.

Hemsworth and South Kirkby railway station

Hemsworth and South Kirkby railway station was on the Hull & Barnsley Railway's Wrangbrook Jn–Cudworth station (Hull & Barnsley main line) and opened in 1891. It closed on 1 January 1932 and was demolished, though the station house survives.

Hemsworth and South Kirkby railway station.

Hipperholme railway station

Hipperholme railway station was opened with two platforms by the Lancashire & Yorkshire Railway on 17 August 1850. Pre-grouping operations were conducted by the London & North Western Railway, post-grouping by the London, Midland & Scottish Railway. The station closed to passengers on 8 June 1953, and to goods in 1966.

Hipperholme railway station.

Holbeck railway stations

Holbeck railway station was unusual in that it had platforms on two different levels, the Holbeck High Level (HL) and the Holbeck Low Level (LL). An explanation of these high and low level stations is eloquently described by David Taylor on the *Lost Railways West Yorkshire* website:

> The High Level station was on a bridge and served GNR and L&Y lines which then continued over a viaduct in to Central Station ... Below it was the Low Level station on the MR lines from Wellington Station to the Aire Valley and the NER New Station line to Harrogate. The primary purpose and usage was as an interchange between the Central Station lines and the lower lines from Wellington and New stations so that passengers could change between these lines without having to cross between the city centre stations.

The low level platforms were closed to the public in 1958, and the high level platforms succumbed to closure shortly afterwards in 1962. The route where trains ran through Holbeck High Level station to Leeds Central station had latterly closed in 1967; the tracks had subsequently been lifted and the bridge carrying the high level track over the low level removed. Trains running along the Airedale, Wharfedale and Harrogate lines still pass over the site of Holbeck Low Level station on their way in and out of Leeds station, although there is no clear indication of the former station that existed on the site.

Holbeck High Level railway station.

Holmfield railway station

The Great Northern Railway began services at Holmfield railway station on 14 October 1878 as the terminus of the line from Queensbury, following delays to the Halifax & Ovenden Junction Railway due to land slips in the Halifax area. It became a through station with the opening to goods of the line to Halifax on 1 September 1879, with passenger services not starting along the entire route until 1 December 1879. It became

Holmfield railway station.

a junction with the opening of the Halifax High Level railway to St Paul's (Halifax) on 5 September 1890. The station boasted three platforms and pre-grouping operations were conducted by the Lancashire & Yorkshire Railway and Great Northern Railway, post-grouping by the London, Midland & Scottish Railway and London & North Eastern Railway. Holmfield closed to passengers 23 May 1955, with goods facilities remaining via Queensbury until 28 May 1956 and via Halifax until 27 June 1960.

Holmfirth railway station

Holmfirth railway station was opened on the Holmfirth branch by the Huddersfield & Sheffield Junction Railway on 1 July 1850. The station was a single platform terminus (with a turntable) and pre-grouping operations were conducted by the Lancashire & Yorkshire Railway. The station closed to passengers on 2 November 1959, and to freight 3 May 1965.

Honley railway station

Currently the line through Honley is a single track, with only one platform in use for both directions. The station is on the Penistone line operated by Northern Rail. Honley railway station dates back to 1 July 1850.

Horbury and Ossett railway station.

Horbury and Ossett railway station
Horbury and Ossett railway station was located on the Manchester & Leeds Railway, which ran along the Calder Valley, establishing a key link between the east and west of the country. The station was opened with the inauguration of the line in 1840, on the west of the Horbury Bridge Road, and to the south-west of the town. Later, a new, more substantial structure was built just to the east. Horbury and Ossett station closed in 1970. Almost all that remains is the old subway which ran under the tracks.

Holmfirth railway station, closed in 1965.

Horbury Junction railway station.

Horbury Junction railway station
The Lancashire & Yorkshire Railway opened Horbury Junction railway station on their new line from Wakfeield to Barnsley in 1850. The station closed on 11 July 1927.

Horbury Millfield Road railway station
Horbury Millfield Road railway station began operations on 11 July 1927 and closed on 6 November 1961.

Horsforth railway station entrance.

Horsforth railway station

In 1969 Horsforth railway station was unstaffed and all the buildings were demolished as part of the general retrenchment of railways in West Yorkshire at that time. Growing traffic congestion in Leeds promoted an increased traffic from Horsforth in the 1990s, and in 2002/3 Horsforth station was extensively redeveloped to better cater for the greater number of passengers. New waiting rooms were built on the two platforms, along with a ticket office on the Leeds (up) platform, which opened on 16 July 2003. The car park was extended and the station is staffed at certain times of the week. Horsforth railway station originally opened in 1849.

Horton Park railway station

Horton Park was on the Queensbury–Bradford section of the Queensbury Lines and opened on 1 November 1880. It closed to passengers in 1952, but remained open to football specials on match days until 1955. The station existed, along with its concrete sign, until recently when it was demolished to make way for a new mosque.

Howden Clough railway station

Howden Clough railway station was opened by the Great Northern Railway on the Adwalton Junction to Wakefield line on 1 November 1866. The station closed on 1 December 1952.

Huddersfield railway station

Huddersfield railway station was designed by the architect James Pigott Pritchett and built by the firm of Joseph Kaye, opening on 3 August 1847. It is well known for its classical-style façade with a portico of the Corinthian order, six columns in width and two in depth. It is a Grade I listed building. The station is managed by First TransPennine Express, who provide trains between the north-east, North and East Yorkshire, Leeds to the east, and Manchester Piccadilly and the north-west. It is also served by local Northern Rail trains on the Huddersfield line, between Leeds/Wakefield Westgate and Manchester Victoria station. Also, the Penistone line to Sheffield (where the Midland main line is reached for services to Leicester and London) and more recently the Caldervale line for trains towards Halifax and Bradford Interchange.

Huddersfield railway station frontage.

Huddersfield railway station interior.

Hunslet Goods railway station

Hunslet Goods railway station was on the Great Northern Railways Beeston Jn–Hunslet Goods (Leeds) line and opened for goods only on 2 January 1899. It closed on 3 July 1967.

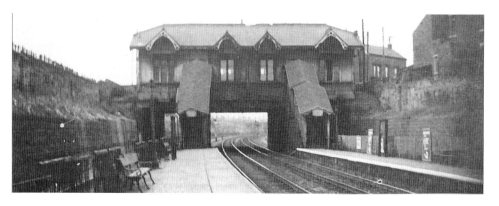

Hunslett railway station buildings.

Hunslet railway station

The first Hunslet railway station opened in June 1854 and closed on 14 September 1873. Another station on Hillidge Road opened on the same day, and on *www. hunslet.org* it is remembered as being: 'Glass, high-vaulted, wood panelled, painted dark green.' The station closed on 13 June 1960.

Idle railway station

Idle railway station was built by the Leeds & Bradford Railway in 1847, but it was closed the following year. On 15 April 1875 another Idle railway station was opened, on the Great Northern Railway's Laisterdyke East Jn–Shipley line. The station had two platforms and was situated south of the High Street, next to the Oddfellows Hall. It closed on 2 February 1931 and little now remains to show that there was ever a railway station in Idle.

Ilkley railway station exterior view.

Ilkley railway station, spring 2000. (*John Law*)

Ilkley railway station

Ilkley railway station was opened as a terminus in August 1865 by the Otley & Ilkley Joint Railway (Midland and North Eastern railways). When an extension to the line opened in 1888 to Skipton via Addingham, Bolton Abbey and Embsay, the station assumed the status of a junction. Terminating trains used the bay platforms 1 and 2, and through lines were served by platforms 3 (in the down direction) and 4 (up). The extension was closed to passengers in 1965 and to all traffic at the beginning of 1966, reducing Ilkley to a terminus once more.

In the late 1980s, the roofed area covering the western end of the station platforms was closed in and converted into a small supermarket, the lines being shortened by around 40 metres to make room for this alteration. The main station building was taken out of railway use and turned over to retail in May 1988. Currently, the station is served by Class 333 electric trains run by Northern Rail, who also manage the station.

Ingrow (East) railway station

Situated on the Great Northern Railway's Keighley–Queensbury section of the Queensbury Lines, Ingrow (East) railway station opened on 7 April 1884. It was only yards away from the Ingrow (West) railway station on the Midland Railway Company's Oxenhope Branch. To cope with all of the production from the mills, the station had a large goods yard. The station closed on 23 May 1955 and along with goods yard, the whole site has now been incorporated into the vast area occupied by Travis Perkins Builders Merchants.

Ingrow (West) railway station

Ingrow (West) railway station, with a single platform, was opened in 1867, along with the rest of the Keighley & Worth Valley Railway line. It closed in 1961 but reopened again in 1968 and was used as an unstaffed request stop, the existing station building having been badly vandalised during the intervening years. Consequently an appeal was made for donations and enough money was raised to buy the station building from Foulridge station on the nearby Skipton–Colne line, which closed in 1959. It had been built in a similar style to the other stations on the Worth Valley line and was carefully demolished and rebuilt at Ingrow, opening in 1989. Today, the station (off South Street, Ingrow) is the first scheduled stop on the line from Keighley railway station.

Ingrow railway station *c.* 1979. (*John Sagar*)

Ingrow East railway station staff.

CHAPTER FOUR

Keighley to Mytholmroyd

Keighley railway station facing in the direction of Skipton.

Keighley railway station

The first Keighley railway station was opened north of the road bridge in March 1847 by the Leeds & Bradford Extension Railway. It was rebuilt on the present site, south of the road bridge, in 1883. Pre-grouping operations were conducted by the Midland Railway, post-grouping by the London, Midland & Scottish Railway. Presently the station is managed by Northern Rail, who operate most of the passenger trains serving it. Electric trains run frequently from Keighley towards Bradford Forster Square, Leeds and Skipton. Longer distance trains on the Leeds–Morecambe line and Settle–Carlisle line also call there. Keighley is also the northern terminus of the Keighley & Worth Valley Railway. The Airedale line runs from platforms 1 and 2 and Keighley & Worth Valley Railway operate from platforms 3 and 4. The Keighley & Worth Valley service runs daily during the summer and at weekends in other seasons. Also, in some areas, the stations retain some of their former architectural features.

Kippax railway station

Kippax railway station began catering for passengers on 12 August 1878 on the North Eastern Railway's Castleford East Jn–Garforth line. The station, constructed in brick and featuring a glass awning, closed on 22 January 1951 and was later demolished.

Keighley railway station *c.* 1993. (Photograph courtesy of *Yorkshire Post* newspapers)

Kippax railway station.

Kirkburton railway station

Kirkburton railway station was opened by the London & North Western Railway on their Kirkburton branch line on 7 October 1867. Plans to extend the line to Barnsley never materialised and so Kirkburton remained at the end of the route, which was primarily used for the transportation of goods. Post-grouping operations

Kippax railway station buildings.

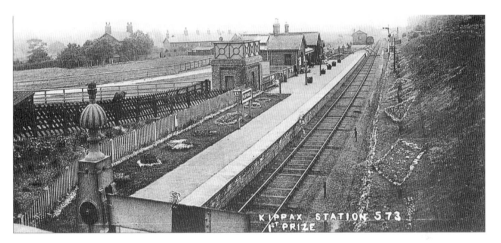

Long view of Kippax railway station.

were conducted by the London, Midland & Scottish Railway and passenger services ran until 26 July 1930. The line continued to be used to transport goods until 1965, when a combination of road haulage and a decline in industry lead to closure. The bulk of the station site is now occupied by a housing development along North Wood Park, which follows the old track bed.

Kirkheaton railway station
Kirkheaton railway station, on the London & North Western Railway's Deighton (Kirkburton junction)–Kirkburton branch line, began services on 7 October 1867. It closed on 28 July 1930 and there is no trace of its former existence.

Kirkstall railway station
Kirkstall railway station was opened by the Midland Railway in 1846 and closed on 22 March 1965.

Kirkheaton railway station.

Kirkheaton railway station.

Kirkburton railway station.

Kirkstall railway station, facing in the direction of Leeds.

Kirkstall railway station.

Kirkstall railway station's stationmaster, Cyril Miles, pictured on the last day of operations in 1965. (Photograph courtesy of *Yorkshire Post* newspapers)

Kirkstall Forge railway station

Kirkstall Forge railway station opened on 1 July 1860 and closed on 1 August 1905. Metro, the Passenger Transport Executive for West Yorkshire, intends to open a new Kirkstall Forge railway station by December 2012.

Knottingley railway station

Knottingley railway station was constructed by the Wakefield, Pontefract & Goole Railway as part of their main line from Wakefield to Goole, which opened in April 1848. In time the station was a busy junction, and became jointly managed by the Lancashire & Yorkshire Railway and Great Northern Railway in 1854. By 1871 the station had lost its trunk line status with the opening of new lines, but it still handled plenty of local passenger and freight traffic (particularly coal from a large number of collieries in the area). The Great Northern made use of its running powers and traffic agreements with the LYR to run through trains from Doncaster to both Leeds and York, putting Knottingley on a new main line between London and York for a number of years until shorter, more direct lines could be constructed. Currently Knottingley railway station lies on the Pontefract line, operated by Northern Rail. Also, the station is the final one in West Yorkshire before the North Yorkshire border and most services terminate (or start) there.

Laisterdyke railway station

Laisterdyke railway station provided passenger facilities from 1 August 1854 as part of the Great Northern Railway's Leeds to Bradford Adolphus Street line. The station had four platforms and closed on 4 July 1966.

Knottingley railway station, 1983. (*John Law*)

Ledston railway station

Ledston railway station, on the North Eastern Railway's Castleford East Jn–Garforth line, opened on 12 August 1878. The station closed to passengers in 1951 and goods in 1969. The station buildings were demolished in 1996.

Leeds Central railway station

Leeds Central railway station was opened on 18 September 1854 as a joint station between the London & North Western Railway, the Lancashire & Yorkshire Railway, the Great Northern Railway and the North Eastern Railway. It replaced the cramped LNW terminus at Wellington Street, which had opened in 1848. Leeds Central was uninspiring architecturally and built above street level. Leeds Central closed on 1 May 1967, when its services were moved to Leeds City station. The last train to leave the station was an early evening service to Harrogate. (Fog) Detonators were placed on the track by railway staff and exploded as the train rolled away from the platform and past the signal box on its final departure. The return trip from Harrogate into Leeds City was without ceremony.

Leeds Central railway station approach *c.* 1868.

Leeds Central railway station staff.

Leeds Central railway station. (Photograph courtesy of *Yorkshire Post* newspapers)

Interior of Leeds Central railway station.

Leeds City station

Leeds City station was born in 1938, when two stations (New and Wellington) were merged together. In 1962 British Railways House (now City House) was added to the station, providing British Railways with administrative buildings. In 1967 a further remodelling of the site took place, when all traffic using Central station was diverted into the City station. At the time of this rebuilding, the station was served by 500 trains on a typical day, with 2.75 million passenger journeys a year. By the 1990s, the station's

Leeds City railway station, 5 July 1982. (Photograph courtesy of *Yorkshire Post* newspapers)

capacity was exceeded on a daily basis, and the 1967 design was deemed inadequate. Thus, between 1999 and 2002, a major rebuilding project took place. This saw the construction of additional approach tracks at the western end of the station, improving efficiency by separating trains travelling to or from different destinations and preventing them from having to cross each other's routes. The station was expanded from twelve to seventeen platforms, with the construction of new platforms on the south side, and the reopening of the now-disused parcels depot to passengers on the north side. The majority of the track, points and signals were also replaced. The 1967 metal canopy was replaced with a new glass roof, considerably increasing the amount of daylight on the platforms, and a new footbridge was provided, replacing the previous underpass.

Leeds Marsh Lane railway station

Commencing services on 22 September 1834, Leeds Marsh Lane railway station was the terminus for the Leeds & Selby Railway's services between Leeds and Selby. For a number of years, Marsh Lane acted as a terminus for railway routes from the east of Leeds prior to the construction in 1869 of the viaduct that now runs through the city centre. The station, resited in 1869, existed until 1958, when it was demolished.

Scene on the platform at Leeds City railway station, 31 May 1955. (Photograph courtesy of *Yorkshire Post* newspapers)

Leeds New railway station

Opening in 1869, Leeds New railway station was a joint enterprise by the London & North Western Railway and the North Eastern Railway. This connected the former Leeds & Selby Railway line to the east with the LNWR lines to the west. A mile-long connection was built, carried entirely on viaducts and bridges. New station itself was built partially on a bridge over the River Aire. It was situated adjacent to Wellington

Leeds New railway station.

station. Following the 1921 Railways Act, when railways in Great Britain were subsequently grouped into four companies, New station remained jointly-operated, but now by the London, Midland & Scottish Railway (LMS) and the London & North Eastern Railway (LNER). Leeds New railway station existed until 1938, when it was merged with Leeds Wellington station to form Leeds City station.

Leeds Hunslet Lane railway station

Leeds Hunslet Lane railway station was opened as 'Leeds' by the North Midland Railway on 1 January 1840. Nine years later, it was renamed Leeds Hunslet Lane. *Wikipedia* provides a description of the station:

> Designed by Francis Thompson, the train shed consisted of an iron roof in four spans, with five lines running into it. Three were stabling lines under the central span, while each outer span had one line with a platform 300 yards (274 m) long. Turntables were provided at each end and the offices on the western side were fronted by an arcade with an arch surmounted with the arms of Leeds, Sheffield and Derby. It was shared by the Manchester and Leeds Railway which ran on the NMR tracks from just north of Normanton since Parliament had refused to sanction two lines running side by side.

Leeds New railway station interior.

It was replaced by the Midland Railway, with Wellington station opening on 30 June 1846, and became a goods depot which closed in the 1980s and the Crown Point Retail Park, which opened in 1989, now lies on the site.

Leeds Wellington railway station

Leeds Wellington railway station was opened on 30 June 1846 surviving until 1938 when it was merged with Leeds New railway station to form Leeds City Station. Part of Wellington station then became a parcel depot.

Leeds Whitehall railway station

During the 2002 rebuilding of Leeds City railway station a small temporary station called Leeds Whitehall was provided to handle some services. This has now been demolished.

Leeds Wellington railway station.

Leeds Wellington railway station.

Leeds Wellington railway station new façade *c.* 1926.

Lightcliffe railway station

Lightcliffe railway station was opened on the Lancashire & Yorkshire line between Halifax and Low Moor on 7 August 1850. It comprised two platforms and post-grouping operations were conducted by the London, Midland & Scottish Railway. The station closed on 14 June 1965. No trace of the buildings remain, but the original flight of stairs from the station into St Giles Road is still in use, giving access to a housing estate built on the station site.

Lightcliffe railway station, situated between Halifax and Low Moor.

Liversedge Central railway station

Liversedge Central railway station was on the Lancashire & Yorkshire railway's Mirfield No. 3–Low Moor (Spen Valley) line and was inaugurated on 18 July 1848. It closed on 14 June 1965 and no trace remains.

Liversedge railway station panorama.

Liversedge Spen railway station

The London & North Western Railway opened Liversedge Spen railway station on their Heaton Lodge–Farnley Junction (Leeds New Line) on 1 October 1900. The platforms and buildings were of timber construction and closure came on 5 October 1953.

Lockwood railway station

Lockwood railway station was opened on 1 July 1850. Currently it is only a single platform station (although the line was once double track). It is situated on the Penistone line between Huddersfield and Sheffield and train services are provided by the Northern Rail franchise.

Liversedge Spen railway station.

Lofthouse and Outwood railway station

Lofthouse and Outwood railway station was opened by the Bradford, Wakefield & Leeds Railway in 1858. It included a wooden building with a glass frontage housing the booking hall, waiting rooms and toilets. It closed on 13 June 1960. Lofthouse station was reopened in 1988 and renamed Outwood.

Lockwood railway station.

Lofthouse and Outwood railway station (Methley Branch)

Lofthouse and Outwood railway station on the Methley Joint Railway's Lofthouse North Jn–Methley Joint Jn opened as Lofthouse Junction on 1 May 1869. It was renamed Lofthouse and Outwood in 1888 and closed on 17 June 1957. Now no trace remains.

Longwood and Milnsbridge railway station

Longwood and Milnsbridge railway station was opened by the London & North Western Railway on their Heaton Lodge to Stalybridge line on 1 August 1849. It closed on 7 October 1968.

Lofthouse and Outwood railway station.

Lofthouse and Outwood railway station staff.

Low Moor railway station

Low Moor railway station, on the Lancashire & Yorkshire Railway's Mirfield–Low Moor (Cleckheaton Branch) line, opened on 9 July 1848. It was closed on 14 June 1965 and demolished.

Luddendenfoot railway station

Luddendenfoot railway station was opened by the Manchester & Leeds Railway on their Calder Valley main line (Manchester to Normanton) on 5 October 1840. Branwell Brontë was employed as a clerk at the station in 1841. It comprised two platforms and closed on 10 September 1962.

Manchester Road (Bradford) railway station

Manchester Road (Bradford) railway station, on the Great Northern Railway's Bradford (St Dunstans)–Keighley line, began services on 14 October 1878. However, competition from trams closed the station on 31 December 1915 and now no trace remains.

Manningham railway station

Manningham railway station was opened by the Midland Railway on 17 February 1868. It was closed to passengers on 22 March 1965.

Marsden railway station

Currently the Marsden railway station has three platforms and is on the Huddersfield Line, operated by Northern Rail. Other than simple shelters on the platforms, there are no station buildings and it is unmanned. The station's former goods yard is now

Manningham railway station.

Luddenfoot railway station, which closed in 1962.

Marsden railway station, 6 April 1992. (Photograph courtesy of *Yorkshire Post* newspapers)

the headquarters of the National Trust's Marsden Moor Estate, and the goods shed contains a public exhibition – 'Welcome to Marsden' – which gives an overview of the area and its transport history. The station was opened by the London & North Western Railway on 1 August 1849.

Marsh Lane railway station (refer to Leeds Marsh Lane)

Meltham railway station
Meltham railway station was opened by the Lancashire and Yorkshire Railway on their Meltham Jn (Lockwood)–Meltham line on 5 July 1869. It was a single platform station and closed on 23 May 1949. The former site is now occupied by a Morrisons supermarket.

Meltham railway station.

Meltham Mills Halt railway station
Meltham Mills Halt railway station was on the Lancashire & Yorkshire Railway's Meltham Jn (Lockwood)–Meltham line which commenced passenger services on 5 July 1869. It was an unadvertised station serving the Union Thread Mills of

J. & P. Coates, later taken over by David Brown for tractor construction. No trace remains of the station.

Menston railway station

Menston railway station opened on 1 November 1875. It was redeveloped in 2000 as part of the general improvements to the Wharfedale line by the West Yorkshire Passenger Transport Executive. The derelict station building was brought back into use and a new ticket office was opened. It is served by Class 333 electric trains run by Northern Rail, who also manage the station.

Meltham railway station, 1945.

Menston railway station, 8 April 1963. (Photograph courtesy of *Yorkshire Post* newspapers)

Menston Junction railway station

Menston Junction railway station, on the North Eastern Railway/Midland Railway Joint Otley–Burley-in-Wharfedale line, opened in 1873, closing in 1877.

Methley Junction railway station

Methley Junction railway station was built by the Lancashire & Yorkshire Railway on its Castleford Cutsyke Junction to Methley Junction line and opened on 1 October 1849. It closed on 4 October 1943 and no trace remains.

Methley railway station

Methley railway station was opened on 1 July 1840 by the North Midland Railway on its line from Derby to Leeds. British Railways renamed it Methley North on 25 September 1950 and closure came on 16 September 1957. However, the stationmater's house survives as a private dwelling and sits incongruously in the modern housing estate which has been built on the site.

Methley railway station.

Methley railway station, 17 June 1980. (Photograph courtesy of *Yorkshire Post* newspapers)

Methley Joint/South railway station

Methley Joint railway station was built by the Methley Joint Railway, which included the Lancashire & Yorkshire Railway, the Great Northern Railway and the North Eastern Railway, on a line from Lofthouse North Jn to Lofthouse Jn

(Methley). The station, opened on 1 May 1869, was known as Methley Joint station until it was renamed Methley South in 1951. It closed on 7 March 1960, but survives almost intact, along with some ancillary buildings, in private ownership, and has been converted to a house.

Micklefield railway station.

Micklefield railway station
Micklefield railway station was opened by the Leeds & Selby Railway in 1834. The original station was replaced around 1880 and it is currently operated by Northern Rail.

Middleton Park Halt
Middleton Park Halt is on the Middleton Railway's Heritage line. The Middleton Railway is the world's oldest continuously working railway. It was founded in 1758 and is now a heritage railway, run by volunteers from The Middleton Railway Trust Ltd since 1960.

Mirfield railway station. (Photograph courtesy of *Yorkshire Post* newspapers)

Mirfield railway station

Mirfield railway station was opened during April 1845 by the Manchester & Leeds Railway and closed on 5 March 1866, being resited. It lost its buildings to demolition in the late 1970s and is currently operated by Northern Rail. The platforms have an unusual configuration. Platforms 1 and 2 form an island platform on the western side of the bridge over Station Road/Hopton New Road. Platform 3 is a side platform on the eastern side of the bridge.

Moor Road railway station

Moor Road railway station is on the Middleton Railway's heritage line.

Moorthorpe railway station *c.* 1981. (*John Law*)

Moorthorpe and South Kirkby railway station

Moorthorpe and South Kirkby railway station was opened in May 1879 jointly by the Midland Railway and North Eastern Railway as part of their Swinton & Knottingley Joint Railway scheme. At the present time it lies on the Dearne Valley line and the Wakefield line, both operated by Northern Rail. A footbridge was opened at the station at the end of May 2010; previously, passengers had to cross the tracks at a flat crossing.

Morley Top railway station

Morley Top railway station, on the Leeds, Bradford & Halifax Junction Railway's Ardsley–Laisterdyke (Bradford) line, opened on 10 October 1857. It closed on 2 January 1961.

Morley Low railway station

Morley railway station was opened by the London & North Western Railway in 1848 as 'Morley Low station.' At the present time the station is operated by Northern Rail.

Scene at Morley Low railway station.

Mytholmroyd railway station

Mytholmroyd railway station was opened during May 1947. It lies on the Caldervale line operated by Northern Rail. Access problems were one cause of closure of the original station buildings, and a new access route, with platforms relocated a few yards to the east, was built by Metro (WYPTE) in the early 1990s. There is an active station user group – Mytholmroyd Station Partnership – that has enhanced the station area with gardens, flower tubs and school art – including the Northern Mosaic by students from Calder High School. The original buildings remain, boarded and unused, and several schemes have been proposed for alternative uses.

Mytholmroyd railway station.

CHAPTER FIVE

Netherton to Ryhill Halt

Netherton railway station.

Netherton railway station

Netherton railway station was on the Lancashire & Yorkshire Railway's Meltham Jn (Lockwood)–Meltham line and opened on 5 July 1869. It closed on 23 May 1949 and the site is now a farm.

New Pudsey railway station

New Pudsey railway station was opened as a new station for Pudsey on 6 March 1967, but it is actually located in Farsley – 1 mile north-west of Pudsey town centre. There is no place called New Pudsey. The station is situated just under a mile west of the location of what was Stanningley (formerly Stanningley for Farsley), which closed on 30 December 1967, having supposedly been replaced by New Pudsey – although the two catchment areas were largely different. The platforms are long enough to accommodate InterCity trains, and there is a large car park, because it was originally served by occasional through trains from Bradford Interchange to London King's Cross. After electrification of the East Coast Main Line, through services were routed via Shipley to Bradford Forster Square. The station is staffed, and at the present time the ticket office is open at regular times during the week.

New Pudsey railway station, 24 January 2007. (Photograph courtesy of *Yorkshire Post* newspapers)

Newtown Goods railway station

Newtown Goods railway station, on the Midland Railway's Mirfield Jn–Huddersfield (Newtown Goods) line, opened on 1 November 1910. It closed on 5 August 1968 and the site has been redeveloped.

Normanton railway station

Normanton railway station, opened by the North Midland Railway in 1840, provided a junction with the York & North Midland Railway and the Manchester & Leeds Railway. Eventually it became the focus of several railway lines and one of the most important stations in northern England – even Queen Victoria stopped over in the Station Hotel. The town also served as an important part of the transport infrastructure for national and local industries, including coal and bricks, although most of this was lost during the 1950s and 1960s. Both express and local trains on the NMR main line ceased to call in 1968 and trains to York ended in 1970, leaving only Hallam line trains to serve the station. It is presently operated by Northern Rail.

Northorpe Station

Northorpe Station was opened on 1 October 1900 by the London & North Western Railway on their Heaton Lodge–Farnley Junction (Leeds New Line). The station buildings and platform were of timber construction, and on 11 July 1921 were destroyed by fire. Later, the station was rebuilt by the LMS on the south side of the Bank Lane bridge and renamed Northorpe Higher to differentiate it from the other Northorpe station, near the Station Hotel, on the Mirfield to Bradford line. Northorpe Higher railway station closed on 5 September 1953.

Northorpe Lower (North Road)

Northorpe Lower (North Road) railway station, on the Lancashire & Yorkshire Railway's Mirfield No. 3–Low Moor line, opened on 1 December 1891. It closed on 14 June 1965.

Normanton railway station, from an old print.

Normanton railway station, 26 January 1972. (Photograph courtesy of *Yorkshire Post* newspapers)

Normanton railway station, spring 1988. (*John Law*)

Normanton railway station demolition, 20 February 1980. (Photograph courtesy of *Yorkshire Post* newspapers)

Nostell railway station

Nostell railway station was opened on the West Riding & Grimsby Railway's line between Wakefield and Doncaster on 1 February 1866. It was built of brick and similar in design to the stations at Hemsworth and South Elmsall, closure coming on 29 October 1951.

Oakenshaw railway station

Oakenshaw railway station opened as 'Wakefield' on the North Midland Railway's Cudworth North Jn–Goose Hill Jn (Normanton) line on 1 July 1840. It was

Nostell railway station.

renamed Oakenshaw in 1841 and underwent several other name variations after that, before closing on 1 June 1870 and being replaced by Sandal & Walton railway station.

Nostell railway station.

Oakworth railway station

Oakworth railway station was originally opened on the Keighley to Oxenhope branch line on 13 April 1867 by the Midland Railway. It closed in 1962 but reopened in 1968, being managed by the Keighley & Worth Valley Railway. The station can still be seen much as it was in the period 1905–10, and is still lit by gas lights both

Oakworth railway station.

inside the buildings and on the platform. It is famous for being the station in the film *The Railway Children*.

Ossett railway station
An Ossett railway station was opened in 1864 by the Bradford, Wakefield & Leeds Railway on their Adwalton Junction to Wakefield line but was renamed Flushdyke, another Ossett station opening soon afterwards. Ossett was closed on 1 September 1964 and demolished. Currently the site is occupied by housing in Southdale Gardens, but the station house survives.

Otley railway station
Otley railway station was opened as a joint venture on the Otley & Ilkley Joint Railway, which was constructed by the North Eastern Railway and the Midland Railway, on 1 February 1865. The station was closed on 22 March 1965.

Outwood railway station
The new Outwood railway station, opened on 12 July 1988, is near the site of the former Lofthouse and Outwood station, which was closed on 13 June 1960. The new Outwood railway station is managed by Northern Rail.

Otley railway station, which closed in 1965.

Otley railway station.

Ovenden railway station

Ovenden railway station, on the Halifax & Ovenden Junction Railway's line from Queensbury to Halifax via Holmfield, Ovenden and North Bridge, opened on 2 June 1881. It was built of timber and comprised two platforms. Pre-grouping operations were by the Lancashire & Yorkshire Railway and Great Northern Railway, and post-grouping by the London, Midland & Scottish Railway and London & North Eastern Railway. The station closed on 23 May 1955. Most of the buildings survive, and are used for light industrial purposes.

The earlier Lofthouse and Outwood railway station

Scene on the opening day of the new Outwood railway station, 12 July 1988.

Ovenden railway station.

Oxenhope railway station

Opening in 1867, and closing in 1962 under the Beeching Axe, Oxenhope railway station was re-opened when the line was preserved in 1968. It is the terminus of the Keighley & Worth Valley Railway, with trains to Haworth and Keighley. Oxenhope houses an exhibition shed, funded by the Heritage Lottery Fund, where some of the locomotives that are not currently used on the line are stored. There is also a station shop, buffet and a car park.

Oxenhope railway station.

Parlington Hall railway station

Situated on the Aberford Railway's Garforth–Aberford line (The Aberford Railway or Fly Line), Parlington Hall railway station opened on 3 August 1837. It closed in 1924.

Pellon railway station

Pellon railway station, on the Joint Great Northern & Lancashire & Yorkshire Railway from Holmfield to St Paul's was opened on 5 September 1890. It was one of

Oxenhope railway station, photographed in 1994. (*John Law*)

two stations on the short-lived Halifax High Level Railway, which was built to serve the west side of Halifax. The branch and its two stations closed to passengers on 1 January 1917, largely due to the introduction of electric trams to Halifax.

Penda's Way railway station
Penda's Way railway station was opened by the North Eastern Railway's Cross Gates–Wetherby East Jn line on 5 June 1939. It had timber platforms, and on the *Barwick in Elmet Historical Society* website there is the following information:

> Mr H. Harding of Swarcliffe recalls how his mother became station mistress of Penda's Way in 1943. Apparently regular passengers helped her to handle the heavy parcels and to release the baskets of homing pigeons, a task she evidently did not relish. The street party celebrations at the end of the war at Penda's Way were threatened by inclement weather and Mrs Harding "saved the day" by opening up the down side (to Leeds) station waiting room to accommodate the partying revellers.

Penda's Way closed on 6 January 1964 and no trace remains.

Pickle Bridge railway station
(see Wyke railway station)

Pontefract Baghill railway station
Pontefract Baghill railway station commenced services on 1 July 1879 and is currently managed by Northern Rail.

Pontefract Monkhill railway station
Opened by the Wakefield, Pontefract & Goole Railway (one of the constituent companies of the Lancashire and Yorkshire Railway) on 1 April 1848, Pontefract Monkhill railway station is currently on the Pontefract line operated by Northern Rail, and is the busiest station in the town.

Pontefract Baghill railway station.

Pontefract Baghill railway station *c.* 1981. (*John Law*)

Pontefract Tanshelf railway station
Pontefract Tanshelf railway station was opened by Metro (West Yorkshire Passenger Transport Executive) on 12 May 1992. It is the most central station in Pontefract and serves Pontefract Races, the racecourse located just down the street from the station. It lies on the Pontefract Line operated by Northern Rail. In the days of coal mining in the Pontefract area, the station served the needs of the local workforce, with regular and frequent services timed for the beginning and the end of mining shifts.

Portsmouth railway station
Portsmouth railway station was opened in 1849 by the Manchester & Leeds Railway on their Copy Pit line. The station was renamed by British Rail to Portsmouth (Lancs) and closed on 7 July 1958.

Pontefract Monkhill railway station *c.* 1981. (*John Law*)

Pontefract Monkhill railway station, 12 February 1970. (Photograph courtesy of *Yorkshire Post* newspapers)

Pool-in-Wharfedale railway station
Opened by the North Eastern Railway on 1 February 1865, Pool-in-Wharfedale railway station was closed as part of the Beeching cuts in 1965.

Pudsey Greenside railway station
Opened by the Great Northern Railway on 1 April 1878, Pudsey Greenside railway station was originally a terminus. It closed on 15 June 1964.

Pudsey Lowtown railway station
Pudsey Lowtown railway station was opened in July 1878 and closed on 15 June 1964.

Left: Pontefract Tanshelf railway station, 1992. (Photograph courtesy of *Yorkshire Post* newspapers)

Below: Portsmouth railway station existed 1849–1958.

Queensbury railway station

Queensbury railway station was located some distance away from the town itself, and at a considerably lower altitude; Queensbury is one of the highest settlements in England, and the station was built at around 400 feet lower than the village. The Halifax & Ovenden Junction Railway opened Queensbury railway station on the line from Queensbury to Halifax via Holmfield Ovenden and North Bridge on Easter Saturday 1879. Eventually there were three approaches to the station (from Bradford, Keighley and Halifax, respectively), and it took on an unusual triangular shape. Of all the stations on the Queensbury Lines, this was the most ambitious.

Pudsey Lowtown railway station.

There were also three signal boxes at the station, one for each junction. The station closed on 23 May 1955 and no trace remains.

Ravensthorpe railway station
Ravensthorpe railway station, on the Lancashire & Yorkshire Railway's Ravensthorpe branch (Thornhill to Heckmondwike) line, commenced passenger services on 1 June 1869. Closure came on 30 June 1952. The station buildings were demolished after being damaged by fire.

Ravensthorpe and Thornhill railway station
Ravensthorpe and Thornhill railway station opened on 1 September 1891. The number of platforms in use at the present time is two and the station is managed by Northern Rail.

The north-eastern side of Queensbury railway station, formerly one of Britain's triangular railway stations.

Pudsey Greenside railway station, closed 1964.

Thornhill railway station, 1989. (Photograph courtesy of *Yorkshire Post* newspapers)

Ravensworth and Thornhill railway station.

Ripponden railway station.

Ripponden and Barkisland railway station

Opened by the Lancashire & Yorkshire Railway on the Sowerby Bridge–Rishworth (Rishworth Branch) line on 5 August 1878, Ripponden and Barkisland railway station had two platforms and post-grouping operations were by the London, Midland & Scottish Railway. It closed on 8 July 1929.

Rishworth railway station

Rishworth railway station was on the Lancashire & Yorkshire Railway's Sowerby Bridge to Rishworth (Rishworth branch) line and opened on 1 March 1881. There was only one platform at the station. Post-grouping operations were conducted by the London, Midland & Scottish Railway; the station closed on 8 July 1929.

Robin Hood railway station
Located on the East & West Yorkshire Union Railway's Lofthouse North Jn–Stourton line, Robin Hood railway station was opened on 4 January 1904. Closure came after a relatively short life span on 30 September 1904.

Rochdale Road Halt railway station
Rochdale Road Halt railway station was on the Lancashire & Yorkshire's Greetland No. 2– Stainland (Stainland branch) line and began services on 1 March 1907. It closed on 23 September 1929.

Rishworth railway station, with only one platform.

Rothwell railway station.

Rothwell railway station

Situated on the East & West Yorkshire Union Railway's Lofthouse North Jn–Stourton line, Rothwell railway station opened on 4 January 1904. It closed after a relatively short life span due to competition from trams on 30 September 1904.

Ryhill railway station

Ryhill railway station consisted of two flanking wooden platforms with wooden buildings, the main buildings being on the Barnsley-bound side. The platforms were linked by a standard footbridge. The station was on the Manchester Sheffield & Lincolnshire Railway's (later Great Central Railway) Lee Lane–Nostell North Jn (Barnsley Coal Railway Extension) line and opened on 1 September 1882. It was renamed Wintersett & Ryhill on 1 March 1927 and was closed by the LNER on 22 February 1930.

Ryhill railway station.

Ryhill Halt railway station

Ryhill Halt railway station was established in an old railway carriage by the Lancashire & Yorkshire Railway on their Shafton Jn–Crofton West Jn (Dearne Valley Junction Railway) line and began passenger services on 3 June 1912. Post-grouping operations were conducted by the London, Midland & Scottish Railway and the Halt closed on 10 September 1951. No trace remains.

Ryhill railway station.

Ryhill Halt railway station.

CHAPTER SIX

St Dunstan's to Yeadon

Saltaire railway station.

St Dunstan's railway station

St Dunstan's railway station was a transfer station so that passengers travelling east/west could change trains without entering Bradford Exchange. It was opened with four platforms on 21 November 1878 by the Leeds, Bradford & Halifax Junction Railway. With the run-down in Queensbury services, patronage of the station fell. Pre-grouping operations were by the Great Northern Railway and it closed on 12 September 1952.

Saltaire railway station

Saltaire railway station closed on 20 March 1965, but was reopened by the West Yorkshire Passenger Transport Executive on 10 April 1984. The current station is unstaffed, and has wooden platforms and no substantial buildings. The original Saltaire railway station was opened on 1 May 1856 by the Midland Railway.

Sandal railway station/Sandal and Agbrigg railway station

Sandall railway station was closed to passengers on 4 November 1957, but was reopened by the West Yorkshire Passenger Transport Executive on 30 November 1987 as Sandal and Agbrigg. The station was originally opened in February 1866 as Sandal and was on the West Riding & Grimsby Joint Railway, which linked Wakefield with Doncaster. In 1923, the line became part of the London & North Eastern Railway before being absorbed into British Rail after nationalisation.

Saltaire railway station, 1991. (Photograph reproduced courtesy of *Yorkshire Post* newspapers.)

Sandal and Walton railway station

Sandal and Walton railway station replaced Oakenshaw railway station, which had existed since 1841. It was opened on 1 June 1870 by the Midland Railway on its Cudworth North Jn–Goose Hill Jn (Normanton) line. The station was of typical Midland brick-built construction, had two platforms and was renamed Walton on 30 September 1951. It closed on 12 June 1961 and a private residence has been built on the site.

The first Sandal railway station.

The new Sandal and Agbrigg railway station, 16 June 1988. (Photograph courtesy of *Yorkshire Post* newspapers)

Sandal and Walton railway station.

Saville Town Goods railway station

Saville Town Goods railway station, situated on the Midland Railway's Middlestown Jn–Dewsbury (Saville Town) line, opened for goods only on 1 March 1906. It closed on 18 December 1950 and the site has been converted for light industrial usage. The MR's goods building survives intact, but it has been partially covered in a modern cladding material.

Scholes railway station

The station buildings of Scholes, Thorner, Bardsey and Collingham (all on the same line) were of similar architectural design. To encourage standards of maintenance, annual competitions were introduced in 1895 for the best-kept wayside station. Scholes gained a British Rail third prize in 1961 for Best Kept Station (under stationmaster Mr D. H. Reed). Scholes railway station was on the North Eastern Railway's Cross Gates–Wetherby East Jn line and opened on 1 May 1876. Closure

Scholes railway station.

Scholes railway station, now the Buffers restaurant, 1 August 1979. (Photograph courtesy of *Yorkshire Post* newspapers)

came on 6 January 1964 and the station buildings are presently occupied by Buffers restaurant.

Sharlston railway station
Sharlston railway station opened in 1869 and closed on 3 March 1958.

Shepley railway station
Shepley railway station is currently operated by Northern Rail, and the layout is slightly unusual in that the platforms are staggered on the opposite sides of a road bridge rather than being located opposite each other like other stations on the route.

Sharlston railway station.

The station was opened by the Lancashire & Yorkshire Railway in 1850 and once had a goods yard, which has now been converted to housing.

Shipley railway station
Shipley railway station is now only one of two 'triangular' stations in the UK – the other being Earlestown station in Merseyside. Ambergate station was previously triangular but only retains one platform and Queensbury station was closed to passengers in 1955. Shipley's platform 3 (on the Bradford-Leeds arm) was lengthened in 1990 to serve full-length InterCity trains. The original Shipley station was built by the Leeds & Bradford Railway and opened in July 1846, being resited in February 1875.

Skelmanthorpe railway station, closed in 1983.

Shipley and Windhill railway station

Shipley and Windhill railway station was on the north side of Leeds Road, west of the Bradford Canal, and less than 300 metres from the existing Shipley station on the Midland Railway. It was opened by the Idle & Shipley Railway on 18 January 1875 and built to the same distinctive pattern as other stations on the line, with a short mitre-roofed tower in the centre. Pre-grouping, the station was operated by the Great Northern Railway, and post-grouping by the London & North Eastern Railway. *Wikipedia* states that it 'may have had several other names: Shipley (Great Northern) and then Shipley (Bridge Street) or possibly Shipley East.' The station closed on 2 February 1931 and the building survives.

Skelmanthorpe railway station

Skelmanthorpe railway station was opened by the Lancashire & Yorkshire Railway on their Clayton West Jn–Clayton West line (Clayton West branch) on 1 September 1879. It closed on 24 January 1983. After closure the line was purchased privately by the Kirklees Light Railway and a 15 ins-gauge steam railway built on the trackbed.

Slaithwaite railway station

Slaithwaite railway station was opened by the London & North Western Railway on 1 August 1849 and closed on 7 October 1968. The present station was opened on 13 December 1982 by Metro (the West Yorkshire Passenger Transport Executive) and is on the site of the earlier station. The station has two platforms, with a car park and bus stop at the approach to platform 2.

South Elmsall railway station

South Elmsall railway station was opened by the West Riding & Grimsby Railway on the line from Wakefield to the Doncaster area on 1 February 1866. It is currently operated by Northern Rail. The station buildings are now demolished.

Slaithwaite railway station.

Opening day on the new Slaithwaite railway station, 13 December 1982. (Photograph courtesy of *Yorkshire Post* newspapers)

Sowerby Bridge railway station

Sowerby Bridge railway station was severely damaged by fire in October 1978 and demolished by British Rail in 1980. The current station, which is not on the original site, was built in 1981, is unstaffed and managed by Northern Rail. The Manchester & Leeds Railway Company introduced passenger services at Sowerby Bridge railway station on 5 October 1840.

Staincliffe & Batley Carr railway station

Staincliffe & Batley Carr railway station was opened by the London & North Western Railway on 1 November 1878. It closed on 7 April 1952.

South Elmsall railway station, facing south.

Stainland and Holywell Green railway station

Stainland and Holywell Green railway station consisted of a single platform to the west of a line curving from north (Greetland) to west (terminus), with a single station

Sowerby Bridge railway station.

building and canopy. It was opened by the Lancashire & Yorkshire Railway on the Greetland No. 2–Stainland (Stainland Branch) line on 1 January 1875. It closed on 23 September 1929 and the site is now occupied by the Brookwoods Industrial estate.

Stanley railway station
The Methley Joint Railway commenced passenger services at Stanley railway station on 1 May 1869. It closed on 2 November 1964 and no trace remains.

Stanningley railway station
Stanningley railway station opened on 1 August 1854 and closed on 1 January 1968.

The only platform at Stainland and Holywell Green railway station.

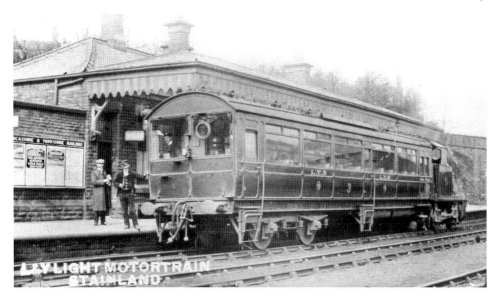

The motortrain at Stainland and Holywell Green railway station.

Stansfield Hall railway station

Stansfield Hall railway station was opened by the Lancashire & Yorkshire Railway on the Copy Pit line in August 1869. The station had two platforms and post-grouping operations were conducted by the London, Midland & Scottish Railway. The station closed on 31 July 1944.

Stanley railway station, facing east.

Steeton and Silsden railway station

The original Steeton and Silsden railway station closed on 20 March 1965, but reopened in 1990. The current (staggered) station platforms are located on the site of the old A6068 level crossing, which was replaced by the current road bridge in 1988 as part of the Aire Valley Trunk Road project. Until closure of the old station both platforms were situated to the north of the former crossing, although the original station building (which survives as a private residence) was located on the Keighley side (south of the current northbound platform). The station and trains serving it are operated by Northern Rail. The original station had opened in December 1847 and was resited on 1 March 1892.

Steeton and Silsden railway station.

Stocksmoor railway station
The number of platforms currently in use at Stocksmoor railway station is two and it is managed by Northern Rail. It was originally opened on 1 July 1850.

Stourton railway station
Situated on the East & West Yorkshire Union Railway's Lofthouse North Jn–Stourton Jn line, Stourton railway station introduced passenger services on 4 January 1904. After a relatively short lifespan, the station closed on 30 September 1904.

Streethouse railway station
Metro (West Yorkshire Passenger Transport Executive) commenced passenger service at Streethouse railway station on 12 May 1992, when the line between Wakefield and Pontefract was re-opened. It has two platforms and is managed by Northern Rail.

Thackley railway station
Thackley railway station closed on 2 February 1931 and presently survives as a residence. Originally, it was on the Great Northern Railway's Bradford (Laisterdyke East Jn)–Shipley line and opened on 1 March 1878. According to Bradford.gov.uk – Thackley, Bradford Potential Conservation Area Report, May 2006, the station was 'rebuilt 1890–1894.'

Steeton and Silsden railway station, 20 June 1973. (Photograph courtesy of *Yorkshire Post* newspapers)

Thackley railway station on the Laisterdyke–Shipley branch line.

Thongs Bridge railway station

Thongs Bridge railway station was situated in a deep cutting, spanned by two bridges at each end. *Wikipedia* states:

> In the original layout, the platforms were staggered either side of Heys Road bridge with the main buildings on the Huddersfield bound platform. This layout was criticised by the Board of Trade after a number of accidents involving passengers. In 1893 the L&YR commissioned Robert Leak & Co to build a new platform opposite the station buildings and increase the gap between the running lines from 5ft 9in to the standard 6ft gauge. 1901 saw the Huddersfield bound platform heightened, a new two storey booking office constructed, and an iron-lattice footbridge built across the line.

The station could be found on the Lancashire & Yorkshire Railway's Brockholes Jn–Homfirth (Holfirth branch) line and opened on 1 July 1850. Closure came on 2 November 1959 and the station was demolished; the site is now covered with housing.

Thorner railway station

Thorner railway station was one of five stations on the North Eastern Railway's Cross Gates–Wetherby East Jn line and began passenger services on 1 May 1876. Thorner closed on 6 January 1964 and the site is now covered with housing.

Thornhill railway station

Thornhill railway station was opened as 'Dewsbury' by the Manchester & Leeds Railway on their Calder Valley main line (Manchester–Normanton) on 5 October 1840. The name was changed to Thornhill during January 1851. Pre-grouping operations were conducted by the Lancashire & Yorkshire Railway, post-grouping by the London, Midland & Scottish Railway. The station closed on 1 January 1962.

Thongsbridge railway station, closed 1959.

Thornton railway station

Situated on the Great Northern Railway's Keighley–Queensbury section of the Queensbury Lines, Thornton railway station opened on 14 October 1878. It had an island platform and was very close to the 270-metre twenty-arch Thornton Viaduct which spanned the Pinch Beck Valley. The station closed on 23 May 1955.

Thorp Arch railway station

Opening on 10 August 1847, Thorp Arch railway station was on the line between Church Fenton and Spofforth and closure came on 6 January 1964.

Thorner railway station.

Thwaites railway station
Thwaites railway station was opened on 1 June 1892 and closed on 11 July 1909.

Tingley railway station
Tingley railway station opened in May 1959 and closed on 1 February 1954.

Thorp Arch railway station.

Todmorden railway station
At Todmorden railway station there is a ticket office on platform 1 and waiting rooms on the two platforms. Also on platform 1 is the Platform 1 Gallery, an art gallery run by Todmorden art group, which has regular exhibitions as well as selling hand-made gifts and other art work. There is also a small library, and a herb garden. Todmorden Station Partnership helps look after the station and stage events. The

station was opened on 3 December 1840 and it is currently managed by Nothern Rail.

Triangle railway station

Located on the Lancashire & Yorkshire Railway's Sowerby Bridge–Rishworth (Rishworth Branch) line, Triangle railway station was opened on 1 June 1865. Operations post-grouping were by the London, Midland & Scottish Railway and the station closed on 6 July 1929.

Upper Batley railway station

Upper Batley railway station was on the Bradford, Wakefield & Leeds Railway (later West Yorkshire Railway, which was in turn was absorbed in by the expanding GNR) on their Wrenthorpe South Jn (Wakefield)–Batley–Adwalton Jn line. The station opened on 19 August 1863. It closed on 4 February 1952; the station house is a modern residence.

Upper Batley railway station facing south.

Upton and North Elmsall railway station

Commencing services on 27 July 1885, Upton and North Elmsall railway station was situated on the Hull & Barnsley Railway's Wrangbrook Jn–Cudworth line. It closed on 1 January 1932.

Wakefield Kirkgate railway station

The original Wakefield Kirkgate station was erected by the Manchester & Leeds Railway in 1840, and it remained the only station in central Wakefield until Westgate began services in 1867. The present building dates from 1854. Some demolition work took place in 1972, removing buildings on the island platform and a roof which covered the whole station. A wall remains as evidence of these buildings, with an original ironwork canopy. Following this, Kirkgate was listed in 1979. The station is owned by Network Rail, with Northern Rail leasing the facilities they use. The station is unstaffed

Upper Birstall railway station.

Upton and North Elmsall railway station.

and served mostly by local trains. Kirkgate station is believed by some to be haunted, with stories circulating about paranormal activity. Apparently, the ghost of a woman in Victorian dress has been seen wandering the subway between platforms 1 and 2.

Wakefield Westgate railway station

Wakefield Westgate railway station was rebuilt in 1967, when a number of the prominent architectural features of the older station were removed. Westgate has become the main station in the city and *Wikipedia* states:

> There are plans to regenerate the entire Westgate area of Wakefield, with the station being moved back down the line to allow for longer platforms to enable two trains to use the platforms at once. This means that express trains will be able to pull into the station as local trains terminate or stop, enhancing the passenger capabilities and train numbers the station can manage.

Wakefield Kirkgate railway station, 29 July 1966. (*Ben Brooksbank*)

Wakefield Kirkgate exterior view.

The station originally opened on 5 October 1857 and was resited on 1 May 1867.

Walsden railway station
Walsden railway station was situated between the level crossing and the north portal of Winterbutlee Tunnel. It was opened in 1845 by the Manchester & Leeds Railway and closed on 7 August 1961. A new station was opened a few yards north of the old station by Metro (West Yorkshire Passenger Transport Executive) on 10 September 1990. It is served by the Caldervale line operated by Northern Rail.

Wakefield Westgate railway station.

Walsden railway station.

Walton railway station
(See Sandal and Walton railway station)

Watson's Crossing Halt
The Lancashire & Yorkshire railway opened Watson's Crossing Halt on their Sowerby Bridge–Rishworth (Rishworth Branch) line on 1 March 1907. From the latter date services on the line were provided by Kerr Stuart motor train No. 1 and trailer, later being replaced by a Hughes steam railcar. Post-grouping operations were conducted by the London, Midland & Scottish Railway and the halt closed on 8 July 1929.

West Vale railway station
Located on the Lancashire & Yorkshire Railway's Greetland No. 2–Stainland (Stainland Branch) line, West Vale railway station opened on 1 January 1875. This short double-track branch line, opening in 1875, was converted to railmotor operation in 1907. West Vale railway station closed on 23 September 1929.

Wetherby railway station (York Road)
Wetherby railway station (York Road) was opened on the York & West Midland Railway Company's Harrogate to Church Fenton line on 10 August 1847. It closed on 1 July 1902. The goods shed remains, situated off York Road in a small industrial estate, and has become a popular dance venue.

Wetherby railway station (Linton Road)
Wetherby railway station (Linton Road) was built on a site cut from a hillside by the North Eastern Railway and opened on 1 July 1902. Closure came on 6 January 1964.

Wetherby Racecourse railway station
Wetherby's Linton Road railway was some distance from the local racecourse, involving a walk of just over 2 miles, thus Wetherby Racecourse railway station opened in 1924. *Wikipedia* states: '[It comprised] a ticket booth of wooden construction, starter signals, a ground frame and a footbridge. It even boasted electrical lighting and its own nameboard.' The station closed in 1959.

Wilsden railway station
Wilsden railway station was on the Great Northern Railway's Queensbury to Keighley line and opened on 1 July 1886. The station had two platforms and a large goods shed. It was the last station to open on the Queensbury–Keighley section of the line. Just along the line was the 270 metre long seventeen arch Hewenden Viaduct. It closed on 23 May 1955.

Wetherby Linton Road railway station.

Wintersett & Ryhill railway station (See Ryhill railway station)

Woodfield railway station
Woodfield railway station opened for only one month in June 1874 on the Lancashire and Yorkshire Railway's Meltham Jn (Lockwood)–Meltham line. The station was to have been called Dungeon Wood and the name-board was actually erected but taken down and changed before services began.

Wilsden railway station.

Woodkirk railway station

Woodkirk railway station, on the Great Northern Railway's Batley–Tingley–Beeston Jn line, opened on 1 July 1886. It closed on 25 September 1939. Freight lingered between Woodkirk and Tingley until 1964.

Woodlesford railway station

Woodlesford railway station opened on 1 July 1840 and information on the excellent website www.woodlesfordstation.co.uk states:

> Woodlesford's station building had a very distinctive design with a square central block and identical wings. It was built from local stone and by the early 20th century was covered in pebble dash which was painted with whitewash. Over the years it turned grey from the smoke of passing trains. One striking feature was that the windows appear to show the building had a first floor above the offices and waiting room. That impression, however, is entirely false and there were never any upstairs rooms. At some point a brick extension with barred windows was added at the rear ... Most of the station buildings on the North Midland were designed by Francis Thompson, notably the rather ornate buildings at Oakenshaw for Wakefield and Cudworth for Barnsley. There were other buildings of a similar basic style to Woodlesford at other stations between Leeds and Derby, for example Wingfield, so it's reasonable to suppose that Woodlesford was also designed by Thompson and erected in time for the opening of the line in 1840...Unfortunately the station building was demolished by British Rail soon after the station became an unmanned halt in 1970.

Wyke and Norwood Green railway station

Wyke and Norwood Green railway station was originally named Pickle Bridge and opened on 7 August 1850. It was renamed Wyke in 1852, moved to the final location in 1896 and named Wyke and Norwood Green. Operations pre-grouping were by the Lancashire & Yorkshire Railway, and post-grouping by the Midland Railway. The station closed on 21 September 1953.

Woodlesford railway station.

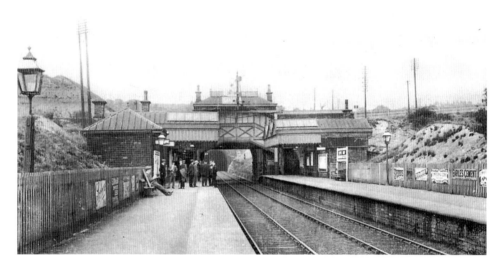

Wyke and Norwood Green railway station.

Yeadon railway station

Yeadon railway station was on the Midland Railway's Guisley (Rawdon Jn–Yeadon (The Yeadon Branch) line which opened on 26 February 1894. The station was only open for goods and excursions, the line closing on 10 August, 1964.